DOMESTIC VIOLENCE

STUDIES IN CRIME, LAW AND JUSTICE

Series Editor: James A. Inciardi,
Division of Criminal Justice, University of Delaware

Studies in Crime, Law and Justice contains original research formulations and new analytic perspectives on continuing important issues of crime and the criminal justice and legal systems. Volumes are research based but are written in nontechnical language to allow for use in courses in criminal justice, criminology, law, social problems, and related subjects.

Studies are both contributions to the research literature and ideal text supplements, and are of interest to academics, professionals, and students.

DOMESTIC VIOLENCE
The Criminal Justice Response

BY

Eve S. Buzawa
Carl G. Buzawa

STUDIES IN CRIME, LAW AND JUSTICE ■ Volume 6

SAGE PUBLICATIONS
The International Professional Publishers
Newbury Park London New Delhi

For information address:

SAGE Publications, Inc.
2455 Teller Road
Newbury Park, California 91320

SAGE Publications Ltd.
6 Bonhill Street
London EC2A 4PU
United Kingdom

SAGE Publications India Pvt. Ltd.
M-32 Market
Greater Kaillash I
New Delhi 110 048 India

Printed in the United States of America

Library of Congress Cataloging-in-Publication Data

Buzawa, Eve Schlesinger.
    Domestic violence : the criminal justice response / Eve S. Buzawa
and Carl G. Buzawa.
       p. cm. -- (Studies in crime, law, and justice ; v. 6)
    Includes bibliographical references and index.
    ISBN 0-8039-3575-7. -- ISBN 0-8039-3576-5 (pbk.)
    1. Wife abuse--United States. I. Buzawa, Carl G. II. Title.
III. Series.
    HV6626.B89   1990
364.1'5553'0973--dc20   90-39605
                                           CIP

Sage Production Editor: Judith L. Hunter

Contents

This book is dedicated to the victims who have long suffered from the violence inflicted in their home. We can only hope that society will begin taking their pain more seriously.

On a more personal note, we are deeply grateful to our children, Aaron and Laura Buzawa, for sacrificing innumerable hours of time together in order for this work to be completed.

Acknowledgments

I would like to extend our deep appreciation to the many individuals whose comments, continued support, and encouragement assisted the completion of this work. Specifically, David Ford, who made extensive comments and suggestions on the manuscript; Gerald Hotaling, who gave considerable assistance with Chapter 2; Murray Straus, David Finkelhor, and the postdoctoral students at the Family Research Lab, University of New Hampshire, for their thorough review and critique of Part II of this manuscript and the use of their extensive resource material; and James Byrne, Peter K. Manning, and Theodore Buzawa for their review of sections of the manuscript.

Naturally, any errors or omissions are the entire fault of the authors.

Eve Schlesinger Buzawa
Carl G. Buzawa

Introduction and Purpose of this Book

What is the appropriate response to domestic violence? This complex question, still without clearly defined answers, is the subject of intense controversy and debate. As such, it has recently become an urgent topic for researchers, practitioners, and other professionals concerned with the study of the family and control of criminal activity.

This book will provide a brief overview of theories of causation of domestic violence and its prevalence in our society. Concentration shall, however, be placed upon the changing nature of how the criminal justice system responds to this problem and the opportunities and limitations of various new approaches being attempted. This work will not try to provide a policy manual or convince readers of the feasibility of a particular approach or set of solutions.

For purposes of this monograph, *domestic violence* will be defined as violence between heterosexual adults who are living together or who have previously lived together in a conjugal relationship. The term is broadly defined and it is acknowledged that definitions are largely dependent on descriptions by the police, assailants and victims, or both. Hence, the definition of family violence is societally based. This adopted definition is "gender neutral" as we see violence as a problem of both sexes (Gelles, 1972; Straus, Gelles, & Steinmetz, 1980). It should, however, be understood that some feminist writers have strongly objected to this perspective believing that it minimizes the disproportionate amount of male violence against women, ignores the "self-defense" aspect of much female violence, and discounts the component of male domination and power at the heart of feminist analysis (Bograd, 1988).

Since empirical research on domestic violence began in the 1970s, it has become clear that without societal intervention, a significant percentage of domestic violence cases escalate into more serious incidents over time. One estimate often cited is that 32% of victimized women will be revictimized within a relatively short time without effective intervention (Langan & Innes, 1986).

Escalation of minor acts of violence occurs when cultural norms forbidding violence in a family setting have, for whatever reason, been neutralized. Subsequent violence becomes permissible or tolerable and often increases in frequency and intensity over time. A history of past violence may also indicate that recurrent violence-provoking factors, such as stress or power struggles, exist within a family so that the family unit is unable to achieve non-violent resolution of these problems. Violence may therefore be used as a successful vehicle to achieve the batterer's immediate ends, that is, of winning a power struggle to dominate the family or perversely to achieve self respect. Unless intervention occurs, the success of violence reinforces the act and increases its pervasiveness in a relationship.

Traditionally, the primary social institution intervening in domestic abuse cases has been the local law enforcement agency. In fact, Dutton (1988) estimated that as many as 14.5% of all actual domestic assaults come into police contact, far more than to any other agency. Widely acknowledged as having a pivotal role, local police departments usually have the initial contact with violence-prone families; provide free service; are highly visible authority figures; maintain a central dispatch system; and are likely to be the only public agency in a position to provide rapid assistance on a 24 hour basis (Bard, 1973; Buzawa, 1979; Parnas, 1967; President's Commission on Law Enforcement, 1967; Wilt & Bannon, 1977; Wolfgang, 1958). The last factor is most significant, as shown in a study of one major city where it was found that only 15% of domestic violence calls were received by the police between 8 a.m. and 5 p.m. on weekdays (Pierce, Spaar, & Briggs, 1988). The remaining 85% of domestic violence calls are made at times when alternative service providers are generally not available.

Even if other services are available, they are not as widely known or accessible to the general public (Hanmer, Radford, & Stanko, 1989). Contact with the violent family by other local government agencies has instead traditionally been dependent upon police suggestions, voluntary referrals, the surfacing of child abuse, or sheer accident.

Prosecutors, in turn, are responsible for the evaluation of police actions when the incident results in an arrest; receiving and assessing the sufficiency of complaints requested by victims; and acting as the state's representative in the formal sanctioning of criminal conduct.

In addition to the direct impact of criminal justice intervention, these agencies indirectly define the parameters of permissible contact by criminalizing violence as out of bounds, thus, condoning behavior that does not result in an arrest or a prosecution (Hanmer, Radford, & Stanko, 1989). Hence, the criminal justice system not only functions as initial respondent, but also shapes the probable future response of other social agencies.

Although virtually all observers acknowledge the importance of the police and prosecutors' roles, by the early 1970s it was widely noted that their practices had been of limited effectiveness. In fact, the criminal justice response to domestic violence has been repeatedly criticized for neglecting opportunities to deter future acts of violence, and a general failure to respond to urgent requests for assistance by victims (Buzawa & Buzawa, 1985; Finesmith, 1983; Hanmer et al., 1989; Langley & Levy, 1978).

While the criminal justice response to domestic violence was clearly not ideal, this did not mean it would be altered. While researchers and practitioners had long acknowledged its role to be inappropriate and ineffective, traditional responses remained relatively unchanged for decades (Parnas, 1967).

Three key problems confronted any advocate committed to changing existing law enforcement and prosecutorial policies. First, police departments as institutions were historically remarkably resistant to change. This makes street level implementation of any directives problematic at best, and of necessity, focuses attention upon the methods used to facilitate actual behavioral changes.

The second problem has been a basic disagreement among the practitioners, researchers, and feminists over the central tenet of police policies. There has been a recurrent exercise of police discretion to avoid arresting domestic violence offenders whenever possible assuming it is allowed and supported by probable cause.

Finally, prosecutors have the same biases as the police. They perceive that use of discretion is an integral component of their job and apply it to filter out cases that lack sufficient public purpose to prosecute. In effect, prosecutorial discretion has historically been used to not only eliminate weak cases, but also those considered unimportant. To the extent that misdemeanor domestic violence is judged to be an insignificant crime, it is not surprising that there is a strong bias to continue dismissal of such cases regardless of any instructions to the contrary.

Despite the foregoing, the criminal justice system has changed structurally and to a somewhat lesser extent, operationally, in response to political and social pressures for a more activist role in handling domestic violence. Before the late 1970s, the statutory structure for handling domestic violence could charitably be described as "benevolent neglect." To the extent that domestic violence was even acknowledged by officials, it was considered only as one of many "family problems." Therefore, state assistance, if any, went to traditional social welfare agencies handling a variety of family problems. Until relatively recently, in the late 1960s, the problem was never formulated as being partially a result of the persistent neglect of government institutions to perform their responsibilities.

Since the late 1970s, an almost unprecedented wave of statutory change has directly tried to alter official responses to domestic violence, mainly by enabling warrantless misdemeanor arrests. During this time, 48 states and the District of Columbia have enacted legislation designed to modify official behavior. Such legislation, often the result of the interplay of pressure from feminist groups, actions of concerned legislators, and professionals in the criminal justice system, has markedly changed the underlying legal philosophy toward the problem of domestic violence.

While differing greatly in their scope and limitations, the new statutes expressly purport to make profound structural change in the response of government agencies to domestic violence. Such changes have primarily been concentrated in three areas: The police response to domestic violence, the handling of cases by prosecutors and the judiciary, and to a lesser extent, methods of educating the public to the problem and providing state funding for shelters and other direct assistance to its victims.

In light of these issues, Chapter 1 will provide a brief discussion of the controversy over the proper framework in which to study domestic violence and what is currently understood about its scope in American society. Chapter 2 will then discuss the historical basis of the "classic" pattern of non-interference. The remaining chapters of Part I will cover the characteristics of traditional policies; the critique advanced by researchers, political advocates, and modern administrators; and the factors that have contributed to the continuation of practices by insular bureaucracies even when these factors are no longer considered viable by their administrators.

In Part II of the book, Chapter 6 traces the external pressures which have led to the changes now being implemented. The remaining chapters present a detailed discussion of major improvements now being adopted or discussed: Removal of procedural barriers to official action, new substantive domestic violence laws, the increased use of arrests and of prior restraints upon known offenders, and the development of court sponsored mediation and counseling programs. Emphasis will be placed not only upon the specific reforms being attempted, but also upon the growing controversy over decisions to remove or sharply limit agency discretion. Similarly, because we believe that administrative/legal pronouncements and statutory changes do not automatically translate into operational alterations, concentration is not only given to the mandate of changes but also upon an assessment, even if preliminary, of the impact such changes have had upon the actual delivery of services.

PART I

The "Classic" Response to Domestic Violence

1

Causation and Scope of Domestic Violence

Theories of causation of domestic violence can be loosely classified into three general categories: (1) individually focused theories, (2) those that examine family structure, and (3) those critically reviewing the legal, religious, and economic basis of how violence is structurally based in society.

To some extent, disputes among theorists who focus upon individual or small group etiology, or micro-analysis, versus those focusing upon societal determinants, or a macro-level analysis, are common in academia. The degree of intense controversy among such scholars may be due to profoundly different assumptions regarding societally defined roles of men and women and the ability of individuals to change behavior in such a context. This chapter does not purport to settle such disputes or argue that any particular analytical framework is superior. However, an initial theoretical grounding in the causation of domestic violence is necessary as particular theories of etiology have become implicit assumptions in certain methods of how the criminal justice system treats domestic violence, the primary focus of this monograph.

INDIVIDUALLY ORIENTED THEORIES

Theories focusing upon the individual assailant examine characteristics of the offender and, to a lesser extent, the victim, that increase the likelihood of domestic violence. These typically focus upon the individual stressors created by poverty and/or unemployment; deep-seated associations between love and violence caused by physical punishment from infancy (Straus, 1980); patterns of poor self-control and low self-esteem (Green, 1984); immaturity, depression, schizophrenia, and severe character disorders (Steinmetz, 1980); efforts to keep control despite poor communication skills;

commission of crimes by the offender outside the family (Hotaling, Straus, & Lincoln, 1989); the ability of assailants to externalize blame by rationalizing their actions and blaming their victims (Dobash & Dobash, 1979; Star, 1982); substance abuse, as it has been found that most domestic violence offenders use illegal drugs or excessive alcohol (Kantor & Straus, 1987); and the occupational environment of the offender, for example, the tasks and ideology of specific occupations that are theorized to predict rates of domestic violence with more accuracy than social class or parental violence (Steinmetz, 1980). It has been noted that minority groups, perhaps because they are subjected to a higher level of stress, higher rates of broken families, or as a correlation with poverty, have had higher rates of domestic violence (Steinmetz, 1980).

Finally, Hotaling et al. (1989) found assault to be a general pattern of interaction that does not limit its victims to family members. They found men who assault children or spouses are five times more likely than other men to also assault nonfamily persons. While this same pattern was found with female offenders, the strength of the correlation was substantially weaker.

One variant of an individual centered approach posits that differences exist between victimized women and others. The suggestion is that certain victim attributes may distinguish victims that report multiple incidents of domestic violence from single-event victims (Pierce & Deutsch, in press; Skogan, 1981; Snell et al., 1964). For example, it has been theorized that although most people modify their behavior to avoid future victimization, repeat victims are, like offenders, unable to change behavior patterns.

For this reason, victims of repeated acts of domestic violence were, in earlier psychiatric-orientated articles, termed to be masochistic (Snell et al., 1964) and in later research were termed to be "trapped" by perceptions of their role (U.S. Department of Justice, 1981, in Pierce & Deutsch, 1989). However, Hotaling and Sugarman (1986) in an empirical analysis of the National Family Violence Resurvey could not find a single risk factor that distinguished female victims of minor violence from female victims of severe violence. Also, such psychologically based theories analyzing victim responses to violence may ignore historical traditions condoning familial violence, the superior economic and physical power enjoyed by most men, and the impact of fear of retaliation if a battered woman tries to leave or alter her relationship with the offender (See especially Graham, Dee, Rawlings, & Rimini, 1988, for analysis of how the battering experience itself may limit her perceived options, and how the psychological effects of being battered situationally create the observed phenomenon).

FAMILY-ORIENTATED THEORIES

Family-orientated research, often conducted by sociologists, uses many of the "individual" variables to explain why a particular family unit explodes into violent behavior. However, the primary focus is upon the determination of characteristics of the family structure that lead to high levels of domestic violence. The family is therefore viewed as a unique social grouping with a high potential for frustration and violence (Farrington, 1980; Straus & Hotaling, 1980).

These researchers often comment upon the irony of a family model that tends to generate conflict and violence while being at least theoretically designed to maximize love and support. This may be partially due to the assignment of family responsibilities and obligations based on age and sex rather than competency or interest.

Societal trends on family structure have also been cited by these research-ers as contributing to increasing levels of domestic violence. For example, the increased social isolation of families in today's society is said to neutralize those inhibitive and supportive agents that might otherwise counteract vio-lent tendencies. Therefore, those families that most lack close personal friendships, typifying a stable relationship, are considered at greater risk of domestic violence (Steinmetz, 1980).

Specific characteristics of a family also have been studied as a predictor of future violence. For example, in separate reviews of risk factors of husband to wife violence, Hotaling and Sugarman (1986) and Sugarman and Hotaling (1989) found that high levels of marital conflict over issues of male alcohol use and control in the relationship was the best predictor of the several risk factors examined in accounting for male violence toward women.

Similarly, the experience of violence in childhood as well as the witnessing of violence between caretakers in childhood have been explored as factors in the use of violence in adult intimate relationships. Several studies have found that the impact of witnessing parental violence in childhood is a stronger predictor of violence in adulthood than the direct experience of childhood violence (Hotaling & Sugarman, 1986, 1990; Pagelow, 1984; Sugarman & Hotaling, 1989). These findings have raised questions about whether children who witness domestic violence are themselves in need of protection, (Jaffe, Wilson, & Wolfe, 1986) as well as about the long-term effects of observing parental violence.

This is the classic "violence-begets-violence" thesis cited in many policy arguments over the need for effective intervention in domestic violence. Interventions that effectively limit or curtail domestic violence will also have primary indirect consequences by limiting the exposure of children to violent role models.

Finally, some researchers have found that much domestic violence may be categorized as a pattern of destructive escalation of violence between battling spouses. Specifically, much domestic violence by males may be precipitated by earlier aggression or conflicts by their partners. One researcher noted that often the husband is violent as a response to "provocative antagonistic" behavior of a spouse (Faulk, 1977). The difficulty in applying this model is that virtually all conduct not immediately acceding to the wishes of the other party might be viewed as provocative or antagonistic. Because this is rarely followed by violence, those instances where violence erupted are not well explained by this model. However, it is clear that violence by one party in a relationship is heavily associated with future violence by the other party. For example, one study has shown that if the husband had not previously assaulted the wife but she had assaulted him (however mild the assault), there was a 15% chance that he would seriously assault her the following year, far higher than normal. Further, increases in recidivism among male offenders have been correlated to the actions of their spouses. A 6% recidivism rate has been reported when the female partner abstained from violence compared to a rate of 23% when the wife used "minor" violence, and 42% when the wife engaged in "severe" violence (Feld & Straus, 1989).

THE FEMINIST PERSPECTIVE ON VIOLENCE

A third approach to examining the causation of family violence uses a macro-level analysis to emphasize the "structural violence" considered endemic against women in Western society. It has been accurately noted that societally sanctioned violence against women has been persistent since biblical times. Christianity, Judaism, and other patriarchical religions have been said to affirm a male-dominated family structure. Women in this model have historically been seen as chattel, unable to manage their own affairs without the strong leadership of an authoritarian family patriarch. The patriarch, in turn, traditionally had the right to enforce male standards of accepted "feminine" behavior through whatever means necessary, including force.

Law, religion, and behavioral sciences were seen to historically endorse the husband's authority and justify his use of violence to punish a disobedient wife (Schecter, 1982; Sonkin, Martin, & Walker, 1985; see also Freeman,

1980, regarding the interplay between the English common law legal system and patriarchical ideology).

In this model, women have tended to maintain the home and family unit while industrialized society does not value such an occupation of time. Both the men and women recognize the economic dependence that leaves women effectively powerless to the whims of their partners (Schecter, 1982). This trend is said also to be reinforced by the solitary confinement of "housewives" in their homes since the "privatized" family structure makes familial violence an individual problem, not a societal one (Schecter, 1982). For such reasons, the United States Commission on Civil Rights in its 1982 report *Under the Rule of Thumb: Battered Women and the Administration of Justice* recognized the historical legal and cultural basis for continued high rates of familial violence in our society.

Still other feminists view American society as being based upon "domination" of one class over another, that is, men dominate women, whites dominate minorities, and the upper class dominates those without resources. In this context, *all* men potentially may use violence to subordinate women. Although recognized that most men do not themselves resort to violence, feminists perceive that as the dominant class, men benefit from women's fear of the potential violence of rape or assaults by strangers *and* by intimates. If we adopt this frame of reference, the study of which particular males or family units succumb to the temptations of using violence is largely irrelevant at best, and at worst, distracts from the overall effort to eliminate sexism in society. As a result, one noted feminist researcher has recently observed there is a division between the feminists who find sexism inherent in our society and "family researchers" who do not consider "gender and power" to be the overarching feature.

The link between violence toward women and sexual inequality finds support in recent cross-cultural research on domestic violence. In a study of 90 small-scale societies worldwide, Levinson (1989) found that violence between family members is rare or nonexistent in 16 of them. In his analysis of these varying cultures, he observed that in addition to the existence of natural support systems, a society-wide emphasis on peaceful conflict resolution, and marital stability, spouses in these peaceful societies enjoy sexual equality. This equality between men and women is reflected in joint decision making in household and financial matters, and the absence of a double standard in premarital sex and other freedoms. Consequently, feminists have argued that a holistic view of our social structure is a better method of analyzing why violence occurs than any examination of the individual circumstances of a particular individual offender or family unit.

SCOPE OF THE PROBLEM

Domestic violence clearly is a major problem in contemporary American society. Estimates of its extent are of necessity but tentative with "official" statistics that tend to be fragmented. However, several facts are clear. Levels of "minor" violence are quite high. One study has estimated that more than 50% of American couples have experienced one or more incidents of assault between partners during the course of a marriage (Feld & Straus, 1989). In addition, public opinion polls indicate that a significant percentage of couples have reported violence during the past year, that is, 10% in one Harris poll (Gelles & Straus, 1985).

Although criminalizing acts of minor violence might be considered an inappropriate overreaction, it is important to understand that these acts may have established an implicit cultural norm of tolerating simple assaults such as slapping, shoving, or throwing objects. This may, in turn, provide the impetus for the pattern of serious violence of substantive concern to the criminal justice system.

Acts of serious violence also occur frequently. The National Family Violence Resurvey (Straus & Gelles, 1988) found that 39% of all violent incidents toward wives were serious, involving punching with a fist, kicking, biting, beatings, and attacks with knives and guns. With the exception of homicide, there are no reliable criminal justice statistics documenting the rate of serious domestic violence incidents. This has made it extremely difficult to develop a statistical base to estimate rates of victimization, and therefore to evaluate whether any particular criminal justice agency is doing an adequate job at representing the needs of victims.

However, data on homicide is more complete and indicates a serious domestic violence problem. Unpublished data from the Supplementary Homicide Report collected as part of the Uniform Crime Reporting Program of the FBI shows that of women who were age 18 or older, 12,582 were killed in one-to-one homicide events during 1980-1984. Of these women, 52% were killed by either a husband, ex-husband, common law husband, or boyfriend (Carmody & Williams, 1987). The reliability of the FBI data may be questioned, however. Departments frequently do not keep track of the nature of violence and may merely rely on indicators such as a common last name as a means of categorizing a relationship.

Other problems with relying solely on police data to define the problem short of homicide have been well documented. Standards for collecting and reporting data are in their infancy. Thus statistics on domestic violence may either reflect the department's record keeping or the experience of its service population (Pierce & Deutsch, 1989).

A second problem with existing data has been noted by Pierce et al. (1988) who has observed utilization of police services by two largely distinct populations of domestic violence victims. The first group will typically contact police on only one occasion. The second are repeatedly victimized and are frequent users of police resources, the "regulars" in police parlance. Raw use of police data confounds estimates to determine the numbers of each distinct subgroup.

Further, individuals frequently go to a variety of service agencies. For example, many victims of intentionally caused injuries seek medical services without filing formal police reports (Barencik et al., 1983, in Pierce & Deutsch). In fact, Pierce and Deutsch (1989) believe it is possible that police departments may be the primary service provider for the *less* serious domestic violence injuries; whereas physicians, especially emergency medical personnel, become relatively more important as service providers when the injuries become more serious.

The lack of continuity in services or record keeping also makes official estimates very suspect. Despite widespread adoption of laws mandating the reporting of domestic violence incidents, there is no effective mechanism to consistently collect data from all public health, welfare, and law enforcement agencies in most jurisdictions.

Finally, classification of calls by police has also been problematic. Assaults frequently receive ambiguous typologies such as "persons investigated" or "services rendered." Police categorized approximately 50% of the 3.2 million service calls Boston received between 1977 and 1982 in such a manner. Alternately, an aggravated assault report may fail to indicate that the assailant was a spouse (Pierce et al., 1988).

Pierce et al. (1988) found a decrease in specific classification by officers compared to 911 operators that may be attributed to officer "downgrading" the various problem calls received. Further, this lack of consistent reporting is more likely if an assault or burglary involves a domestic problem or if there have been previous requests for police assistance. The most sophisticated attempts currently in use to identify patterns of repeat service calls to a particular household, as conducted by Pierce et al., may themselves be subject to challenge. Such analysis tends to rely upon street addresses rather than individual names. It can be argued that due to neighborhood characteristics, specific addresses will always contain families at high risk and heavy occupant turnover as opposed to recidivism of a particular familial unit. This may partially account for repeat calls.

As a result of problems with official data, unofficial but quite sophisticated research currently provides the best estimate levels of serious acts of domestic violence in American society. One study, based on self-reports, and

therefore probably somewhat prone to underreporting, estimated that approximately 16% of American couples have been involved in incidents of family
violence, which included punching, kicking, and attacks with an object or a
weapon (Straus & Gelles, 1986). Even if not underreported, this would result
in approximately 8.7 million assault victims.

The high numbers of assaults have unquestionably resulted in massive
numbers of injured and dead victims. It has been estimated that each year,
acts of domestic violence account for approximately 1.5 million women and
500,000 men that require medical attention, more than half of which necessitate hospital visits or stays (National Clearinghouse on Domestic Violence,
1980; Straus, 1986). Finally, domestic violence appears responsible for
approximately 4,400 deaths of family members. In one year, 1984, 24% of
United States homicide victims were related to their assailants, and half of
these, or 12% of the total United States homicide rate, were spouses (Straus,
1986).

Incidents of domestic violence are not merely a problem of one particular
social class. Although most criminal justice involvement has been with the
lower socioeconomic groups, numerous researchers have noted that while
the stress of being indigent, the relative lack of adaptive non-violent skills,
and increased rates of substance abuse may result in higher levels of domestic
violence in lower socioeconomic groups, acts of familial violence are by no
means restricted to this group (U.S. Attorney General's Task Force on Family
Violence, 1984; Bassett, 1980; Coates & Leong, 1980; Ferraro, 1989a; Hart
et al., 1984).

2

Historic Intervention by the Criminal Justice System

To varying degrees, domestic violence has long been both a feature and concern of society. Since ancient times, the patriarch of a family was given the right to use force against women and children under his control (see especially Martin, 1985, for a discussion of familial violence from Ancient Greece to the present). The Old Testament explained and condoned such violence on the basis of women being the "source of all evil." This pattern was recognized by English common law where well-recognized custom dictated that husbands "dominate" wives using violence, "with restraint," for example, the theory of "moderate chastisement." Early English laws amplified on the Common Law. One eighteenth-century law "limited" the husband's right to punish his wife to "blows, thumps, kicks or punches in the back which did not leave marks" (Dobash & Dobash, 1979).

Other societies adopted similar theories. For example, a sixteenth-century Russian ordinance expressly listed the methods by which a man could beat his wife (Quinn, 1985). When the violence became too serious, laws against assault and battery were typically not invoked. Instead, informal sanctions such as social ostracism, lectures by the clergy, or retaliatory beatings of an offender were undertaken by family, friends, the church, and perhaps, vigilantes (Pleck, 1979).

Several excellent articles by Pleck (1979, 1989), discuss how certain of the more religious American colonies began to set more definitive boundaries to accepted permissible levels of violence against other family members. At early as the mid-1600s, several Puritan settlements, the Massachusetts and Plymouth colonies, apparently adopted the first laws in the world that restricted unnecessary violence toward women and children.

However, the limitations of this period of societal intervention should be clearly understood. Puritans did not object to moderate violence as the family patriarch had not only the responsibility but also the duty to enforce rules of conduct. Moderate force would therefore be considered necessary and proper to make certain that women and children in the patriarch's control would follow the correct path to salvation (Koehler, 1980; Pleck, 1979).

Also, as Pleck (1979) and others have noted, the effect of these laws was largely symbolic, defining acceptable conduct and not often enforced by the public floggings or the other more draconian criminal justice punishments then in vogue. In addition, these statutes were confined to the Puritan colonies and not extended to the larger more representative Southern and mid-Atlantic settlements. Finally, as these were primarily based on religion, determining the appropriateness of conduct suitable in the "eyes of the Lord" became even more problematic as society became more secularized. For these reasons, enforcement of these laws largely disappeared by 1700.

During the period between the late 1700s through the 1850s, there were virtually no initiatives by the criminal justice system to control domestic violence, and a legislative "vacuum" existed (Pleck, 1989). In fact, in the early 1800s, judges commonly dismissed those infrequent charges in court decisions because a "husband was legally permitted to chastise his wife without subjecting himself to vexatious prosecutions for assault and battery" (Lerman, 1981). Similarly, another court ruled that a husband could beat his wife with "a rod not thicker than his thumb," for example "the rule of thumb".

It is unclear why such a long period of non-enforcement occurred. It is indeed probable that as society became more secularized, the enforcement of community moral standards in private conduct was actually considered an improper overreaching use of government (Hartog, 1976). It is of course a possible rival hypothesis that levels of domestic violence actually declined during this period. However, there is no evidence that this occurred, and it would intuitively appear unlikely given that the period was characterized by rapid social change and economic dislocations, factors that have been previously associated with higher levels of domestic violence.

Instead, the legal systems of both Great Britain and the newly liberated colonies began to reflect the teachings of "liberal" philosophers such as Locke, who strongly believed that society should restrict its concerns to the maintenance of "public order" and abjure both trying to regulate "private order" or eliminate "private vice" (Pleck, 1989).

The second period of criminal justice enforcement against domestic violence occurred in the context of the major societal upheavals of the latter part of the 19th century. At that time, the middle class became frightened over what they perceived as an uncontrollable crime wave exacerbated by waves of immigrants sharing markedly different cultural backgrounds (Boyer, 1978).

Concerns were also expressed by the nascent women's advocacy movement. Temperance Leagues had a mission to stamp out the most visible cause of societal problems, "demon rum." Growing numbers of suffragettes organized activities designed to help women by lifting numerous restrictions on their freedom, including the right to vote, own property, and of more direct import, not to be considered as legal "chattel" of their husbands. These efforts did affect society's official attitudes toward domestic violence. By the end of the 19th century, "chastisement" as a defense to a charge of assault ended. Twelve states considered and three adopted a stronger position with explicit anti-wife beating laws. In these three states, Maryland (1882), Delaware (1881), and Oregon (1886), the crime of wife beating was officially punishable at the whipping post.

Although these statutes demonstrated societal concerns, researchers now believe that they were rarely officially enforced (Pleck, 1989). Of perhaps more direct impact, vigilantes, including the Ku Klux Klan, supplanted official sanctions by using beatings against alleged offenders, primarily blacks, to explicitly control such behavior. This naturally also had the desired effect of maintaining such vigilantes' claim to dominance as the final arbiter of permissible conduct.

Although it would be easy to dismiss the relevance of this early period to the study of how the criminal justice system currently functions, several recurrent patterns of interface between domestic violence and the criminal justice system appear to carry over from this period. First, laws nominally on the statute books were not equated with real enforcement policies. Although they might exist, criminal sanctions were actually infrequently imposed. Instead, they were tacitly deployed to control the fringes of clearly improper conduct where the excess became impossible to ignore due to a victim's recurrent severe injuries or public breaches of the peace. Informal methods of control instead became the primary vehicle for enforcing basic societal norms.

Second, when official punishment was deployed, it was used far more against blacks, vagrants, and other groups without social power. In this case, it is unclear whether the criminal justice system was primarily involved out of a concern to assist the wives/intimates of these men, or was intended to be an additional vehicle for enforcing the social order against the males.

Third, the contemplated use of the highly visible and emotionally charged whipping post, even though an infrequent occurrence, may be considered an attempt to deter future criminal activity by the prospect of *public* humiliation. As such, it may have been the logical antecedent for modern efforts to use a mandatory arrest policy as a mechanism for deterrence via the prospect of public humiliation, rather than using the nature of the crime itself as a justification for the punishment.

By the early 1900s, the second great experiment of using the criminal justice system to combat domestic violence ended, and by several accounts domestic violence as a legally sanctioned crime virtually disappeared (Pleck,

1979, 1989; Rothman, 1980). This was probably inevitable. Other issues became the focal point of concern by the middle class. Also, most female activists concentrated upon their primary goal of achieving suffrage and subsequently became very concerned with the temperance movement. In the interim, the criminal justice system itself was rapidly evolving away from enforcing crimes of this nature. Political theorists instead began to fear the possibility of coercive use of the police, a trend rapidly increasing in authoritarian states of that era. This, in turn, helped develop rationales for societal respect of "family privacy," traditionally the rallying cry for those seeking no criminal justice involvement in domestic violence (Rothman, 1980).

In this context, case law and statutory restrictions rapidly began to develop that severely restricted the previously largely unfettered powers of the police. In one directly relevant development, virtually all states codified common law that forbade police from making arrests in unwitnessed misdemeanor cases. Finally, the courts, influenced by the nascent social work movement, began viewing the criminal prosecution of domestic violence cases as being "unprofessional." The rehabilitative model used by social workers trying to help dysfunctional family units, or rehabilitate an offender's behavior, was viewed as vastly superior. This era, in turn, has also had a profound impact upon current criminal justice operational practices. To date, and despite official policies to the contrary, many police officers and prosecutors strongly believe that society should not intervene in domestic disputes except in cases of extraordinary violence.

Until comparatively recent times, the procedural requirements adopted by bureaucratized and highly controlled police forces resulted in sharply limited ability to use formal sanctions. There was a concomitant increase in the tendency to mete out street-level justice to minor miscreants, such as giving "stern lectures" or even an occasional beating of drunk domestic violence offenders to "teach them a lesson." Restrictions on warrantless misdemeanor arrests were probably the key factor in this regard. Moreover, restrictive policies of prosecutors adopted in the 1900s also made use of criminal sanctions even more problematic. The combined effect of these procedural barriers made the actual intervention of the criminal justice system far more of a remote possibility to any particular offender and victim than the crime would otherwise warrant in terms of victim injuries or the type of conduct of an offender.

3

The "Classic" Police Response to Domestic Violence

For the reasons discussed in this chapter, police have had little motivation to intervene in domestic violence cases. When intervention occurs, it has been perfunctory in nature, dominated by the officer's overriding goal—to extricate himself from the dangerous and unpleasant duty with as little cost as possible, and to reinvolve himself with "real" police work. It is acknowledged that attitudinal and structural changes are occurring in many police departments. Therefore, it may risk over-generalization to find at this time a "classic" police response.

OFFICER'S PERCEPTIONS OF REAL POLICE WORK

A primary problem has been that most police officers simply do not believe that responding to domestic violence calls is an appropriate police responsibility. They clearly prefer law enforcement functions where the prospects for "action" and an arrest are higher. In contrast, they almost uniformly dislike tasks that imply an additional social worker type of role. The fact, of course, is that police officers have a variety of non-law enforcement tasks where the use of arrest powers would clearly be inappropriate or at least highly unlikely. Such duties include performing rescues, providing transportation to hospitals, and delivering of subpoenas and warrants.

Similarly, police officers perform a variety of tasks in low-level dispute resolution such as intervening to "tone down" loud parties, taking care of the drunk and homeless, and intervening in most "family disputes." In these tasks, arrest powers may be only an infrequently used tool of last resort, and the prospect of "action" sufficient to relieve chronic boredom is highly unlikely. As Manning (1978) observed, officers perceive their job in legalistic terms. While laws and department policies provide the basis for decision making, they generally do not formally address order-maintenance issues.

Regardless of reality, it has long been noted that police are socialized from their earliest occupational training into a culture that doesn't highly value "social work" roles (Bard & Zacker, 1974). A new recruit, to be an accepted member of the police, that is "one of the boys," has meant he must adopt the occupational code (Punch, 1985), including the key elements of protecting other officers, admiration of a "good pinch" by a fellow officer (Van Maanen, 1978), and explicit acceptance of the same normative framework as other officers as to what constitutes a "serious" crime (Stanko, 1989).

It should be noted that the actuality of the police experience is far different than the mythology created by the occupational culture. Specifically, the model of the police officer as "crime fighter" and "law enforcer" has been repeatedly challenged by experienced researchers. They note that making arrests is a rare occurrence (Reis, 1971; Van Maanen, 1974), even though symbolically important in an occupation where the daily activities tend to be dull and repetitive (Berk & Loseke, 1980-1981). The importance of the police self-image, therefore, lies less on the reality as upon the efforts made by many police to undertake conduct consistent with the image of being a "crime fighter."

As a corollary to the above, most officers instead continue to judge each other's competence on the basis of performing crime-fighting tasks such as the apprehension of acknowledged criminals. They do not highly value or even see cases when a successful intervention in a private dispute might have meant that the officer had effectively diffused a volatile and dangerous situation (Stanko, 1989).

The impact of this occupational code is very important to understanding resulting police practices. Obtaining and keeping informal prestige or status with peers is imperative to most police officers. As Manning (1978) stated,

> his most meaningful standards of performance are the ideals of his *occupational culture*. The policeman judges himself against the ideal policeman as described in police occupational lore and imagery. What a "good policeman" does is an omnipresent standard. (p. 11)

Further, rank and file officers have classically maintained a closed internal culture with strong elements of antipathy toward the public at large, politicians, and often even their own command (Manning, 1978; Punch, 1985; Radford, 1989).

Using this frame of reference, the response to a domestic violence call has little occupational value to an officer. It does not give him a chance to protect his compatriots, and most officers don't view the crime as serious. Arrests have typically been infrequent, and since the offender is known and it is a "minor" crime, any arrest that results from the intervention would be considered a "garbage arrest," not worthy of recognition (Stanko, 1989).

WHY POLICE DETEST DOMESTIC VIOLENCE CALLS

Simply understanding that police believe domestic violence calls do not constitute "real" police work does not explain why most police readily state that domestic violence calls rank among the worst duties they face. Instead, we must examine several key factors that have reinforced the almost universal police dislike for responding to such calls.

Organizational Disincentives

There are few formal organizational incentives for good performance of this work. To the extent they are governed by civil service and not the whim of superior officers, typical police promotional practices measure easily quantifiable skills such as arrest rates and subsequent clearances. Similarly, written tests for promotion heavily emphasize textbook knowledge of law enforcement tasks such as substantive criminal law, criminal procedures, and departmental policies regarding arrests and case documentation. Officers are expected to incur no blemishes on their record by exposing themselves or the police department to civil suits or citizen complaints.

In effect, these evaluation criteria may be seen to provide a major, if unintentional, *disincentive* for performing domestic violence tasks. If an officer spends the necessary time to adequately handle a domestic assault case and substantively assists a victim with referrals, he lessens the chance that he will have a major felony arrest by having used his time "unproductively" in an organizational sense. He also increases the likelihood that the offender, or even the victim, might file a complaint based upon his "overzealous" or "overbearing" conduct.

Is the Work Extraordinarily Dangerous?

Officers universally cite their extreme danger when responding to domestic violence calls. They are vaguely aware of statistics that "demonstrate" that officers responding to family disturbance calls are the most likely to be killed or injured. Of more impact are the frequently heard officer "war stories" recounting the incidents where a victim, whom they or the officer in question has sought to help, has "turned" on an officer and bit, slapped, hit, stabbed, or shot him. While they may instinctively realize that many other activities, such as responding to robberies, gang fights, or drunken brawls, are more likely to cause injury, their indignation toward the victim's "fickle" response is remembered with a measure of bitterness that is difficult to overstate.

Until recently, the FBI published statistics that reported the category of "responding to disturbance calls" as responsible for most officer deaths (Garner & Clemmer, 1986). Family violence researchers such as Straus, Gelles, and Steinmetz (1980) also noted the danger in responding to family violence disturbance calls.

The prospect of danger has certainly been emphasized by police departments. The authors have previously been involved in observing and modifying the content of police training programs. Without exception, these programs have placed extreme emphasis upon the inherent danger of the call to the police. They also make frequent exhortations to the effect that if the officer does *not* follow standard procedures, he is dramatically increasing his own chances of injury or death.

While very important for its impact upon police perception, it should be stressed that the fear of injury may be overstated, if not totally misplaced. The reality of the danger to police has been strongly questioned. The aforementioned Garner and Clemmer study (1986), demonstrated that the methodology used in the composition of the FBI statistics had resulted in an overstatement of approximately three times the real rate of police injuries and deaths related to domestic violence efforts. This occurred because until 1981, FBI statistics had collapsed the substantive categories of officers responding to domestic violence calls, bar fights, gang activities, and the restraint of deranged people into the generic "disturbance category." Not unexpectedly, all of the other components of the "disturbance category" generated far higher rates of officer deaths. By separating these components, it was shown that in the years 1973-1982 there were only 62 domestic violence-related officer deaths out of 1,085 officers killed in the line of duty. Given the proportionately higher amount of time that officers spend responding to domestic violence calls than to other activities in the "disturbance category," responding to domestic violence calls does not appear to constitute an especially dangerous activity to police.

Officer deaths may be viewed as being a limited measurement of a call's danger, because the occurrence is relatively infrequent. Assaults upon officers are far more common. However, it may be assumed that domestic assailants are also less likely to use a deadly weapon in the presence of an officer than, for example, a robbery suspect or a deranged individual. This increases the probability that officer injuries have also occurred less frequently in the context of domestic violence than in other "disturbances." For this reason, although it is possible that the precautions taken due to concern over the "danger" of domestic violence may have reduced the numbers of officer injuries, it does seem evident that police overly emphasize the potential for injury in such cases.

Regardless of reality, the effect of such perceptions is regrettably clear. Fear of injury reinforces the dislike of such calls for both officers and command officials. When officers respond to a domestic violence call, they have usually been instructed to emphasize the adoption of a defensive/reactive strategy to protect their own safety. Under such circumstances, it is not surprising that innovations in police responses or a more activist approach have been discouraged.

Is the Police Job Futile?

Traditionally, in many jurisdictions, police attitudes are reinforced by their frequently accurate perceptions that few domestic violence cases brought to court via an arrest or citizen complaint have resulted in successful prosecutions. They are aware that many victims drop charges, that prosecutors often exercise prosecutorial discretion and decline to proceed, or on occasion, that charges are deferred pending a successful diversion program. A case that is actually adjudicated seldom results in conviction with jail time. In an occupational subculture that highly values a "good bust" or a "good pinch" and a formal organization that zealously monitors clearance and conviction rates of officers, domestic violence cases that historically lack such attributes are unlikely to be accorded high status.

Regressive and Fatalistic Attitudes

Some officers themselves may share common community sentiments that domestic violence and other "private misconduct" should not be subject to public intervention. While this has been ascribed to rampant sexism among officers or their own tendencies toward condoning familial violence (Schecter, 1982), we believe the phenomenon is more complex.

In modern times, the police have repeatedly been made painfully aware of significant legal limits to their own use of power. Common examples are in the use of force to extract statements from suspects or the ability to conduct search and seizures on private property. As a result, they are sensitive to an offender's potential claims of violations of his or her constitutional rights. It is not surprising that officers would tend to be more comfortable with the public order/private dispute dichotomy typified by their preferred response to domestic violence.

HAS CLASSIC TRAINING MADE THE PROBLEM WORSE?

The process of police training has been regarded as a primary vehicle for changing existing practices and promoting more desirable attitudes and conduct reflective of the goals of the organization's leadership. For a variety of reasons, the training actually used in domestic violence has not accomplished this goal. Indeed, historically it may have thwarted earlier efforts to implement more progressive policies. Manning and Van Maanen (1978) discuss the importance of the academy in the police socialization process. Occupational perspectives are transferred to new recruits, and course content is presented in such a way as to ensure its continuance.

Police departments typically rely upon an extensive routinized training program of 8 to 12 weeks to impart basic knowledge of substantive criminal law, criminal procedure, and departmental regulations and operating guidelines to their recruits. Before such training, the recruit does not generally have arrest powers. Even after the formal training program, officers are on "rookie" status. In larger departments, these rookie trainees are subsequently assigned to patrol with more experienced officers for weeks or months until they are considered sufficiently familiar with their required job tasks and departmental operations.

In the past, every component of the training process—time allocation, instructor selection, content, and in-service traineeship—tended to reinforce the existing negative stereotypes against domestic violence cases. Harris (1973) has observed that in classic police academies, great emphasis was placed on the "ethic of masculinity" and development of the officer's identity as "first and foremost . . . a man" (p. 291).

In the late 1970s, when assisting the Detroit Police Department in the development of a new training program, the authors conducted a nationwide review of existing domestic violence programs. At that time, the domestic violence-related component of virtually all police training programs examined was perfunctory in nature, usually comprised of a single 4-to-8-hour lecture segment under the general rubric of handling "disturbed persons" (Buzawa, 1978). The content was not restricted to, nor even necessarily addressed, the topic of domestic assault. Instead, it typically included proper techniques for handling hostage situations, potential suicides, mentally disturbed individuals, violent alcoholics and addicts, and child abuse with brief mention of domestic disturbance calls. To the extent they were separately addressed, "domestic calls" were explained to the recruits as a largely unproductive use of time, ineffective in resolving a "family" problem, and potentially dangerous for the responding officer. Recruits were told that the desired outcome was to restore peace and maintain control as a vehicle of restoring the public order and a mechanism for self-protection. Arrests were actively discouraged as a waste of time except when disrespect or threats by an offender or victim indicated that the officer might lose control of the situation. Arrest is therefore assertion of authority rather than a response to the demands of the situation.

Departmental choice of training staff does did not usually result in interested or qualified instructors. Except for those few major departments with a dedicated permanent training section, police academies have traditionally utilized senior line personnel. Frequently, the basis for their selection is a temporary disability or leave or other special duty restrictions, such as having been involved in a prior shooting or other incident requiring a departmental investigation before placing the officer back on active duty. These instructors had little real interest in training itself, generally lacked any instructional background, and had little substantive expertise or affinity for the topic of domestic violence. As a result, it is not surprising that the primary mode of instruction was an explanation of official policies of "non-intervention" accompanied by colorful stories about their own personal experiences. Few, if any, training materials or multimedia aids were available or used, and outside expertise was rarely sought.

Formal in-service training rarely existed prior to the early 1980s. The field training process, where the rookie was assigned to learn under the direction of an experienced officer, usually reinforced nascent prejudices against domestic violence intervention. In fact, this experience served to undermine an academy's instruction in those few cases where the academy might have attempted to promote a more activist police response (Van Maanen, 1973).

This has been an important and largely unrecognized factor that slowed the implementation of change desired by command officials. It has previously been shown that the attitudes inculcated during the field training process can significantly modify or distort instructions from a police academy (Van Maanen, 1974). During the initial entry period, the recruit relies on the perceptions of relevant teachers, such as experienced officers, to develop his own views toward proper organizational practices and objectives. The trainee, after all, has few, if any, other relevant experiences to guide his behavior during a sometimes frightening immersion into the reality of policing (Van Maanen, 1975). Therefore, field training with older officers has primarily served as reinforcement for prejudice against actively handling domestic violence cases.

For these reasons, it has been acknowledged by both senior police officials (Bannon, 1974) and researchers (Loving & Quirk, 1982) that traditional police training has failed to provide police officers with any rudimentary skills required for successful domestic violence intervention. In one relatively recent study, 50% of the officers in a department were not even aware of the elements of probable cause for domestic violence assault (Ford, 1987). Bannon (1975) observed that "the real reason that police avoid domestic violence situations to the greatest extent possible is because we do not know how to cope with them."

Classic patterns of training may therefore be seen to have reinforced prevailing occupational ideology toward domestic violence. The net effect of such a training process was to enhance the likelihood that the officer would attempt to either avoid a response or rapidly complete domestic violence calls in order to devote energy to the more familiar areas considered appropriate police work.

STRUCTURAL IMPEDIMENTS TO POLICE ACTION

Traditionally, there have been a number of structural impediments to appropriate police responses in this area. One severe handicap has been the statutory restriction that peace officers have only the authority to make arrests for misdemeanors upon the prior issuance of an arrest warrant. In effect, this required a prior action by a magistrate or justice of the peace, or allowed action only in those few cases where a misdemeanor was committed in the officer's presence. This is in sharp contrast with statutory authorization of warrantless arrests in felonies. In such cases, an officer only needed probable cause to believe a crime was committed by the suspect rather than requiring that it actually be witnessed by the officer.

Domestic violence has usually been characterized as simple assault, a misdemeanor, unless accompanied by aggravating circumstances such as use of a weapon, intent to commit murder or to inflict grievous bodily harm, or a sexual assault. Therefore, until recently, police officers were legally unable to make warrantless arrests unless the violence continued in their presence or a previously existing warrant had been issued. Prior issuance of arrest warrants was never widely used to prevent future acts of domestic assault. They were limited by being related to specific past conduct, requiring victim initiation, having only a brief period of time until expiration, and necessitating subsequent repeat visits to sign complaints and affidavits to force recalcitrant bureaucracies to act.

In addition, officers have not typically had knowledge when responding to a recidivist family, or a "regular" in police parlance. Information systems and record keeping for dispositions short of a conviction frequently did not exist in any form, or if so, were not readily accessible to patrol officers. When there were convictions, incidents of family violence or disturbances have not systematically been recorded by police departments (Hammond, 1977; Pierce & Deutsch, 1989; Reed, Fischer, Kantor, & Karales, 1983). Under these circumstances, many incidents of recurrent abuse are seen as isolated, unrelated occurrences not necessitating a tough response by police (Pierce & Deutsch, 1989).

For these reasons, a responding officer had little opportunity to determine if a family had been involved in similar acts of violence unless he was intimately knowledgeable with the precinct's problem families. Thus, repetitive spouse abuse might erroneously be thought to be an unusual occurrence not meriting arrest. This problem has been exacerbated by the fact that victims frequently called multiple agencies for assistance in a vain hope for help, therefore preventing any single agency from recognizing the extent of calls for assistance from a particular family.

Finally, the sheer volume of domestic violence cases has been cited as creating an organizational challenge to chronically understaffed, overworked departments. Disputes and disturbance calls are the single-largest category of calls that police receive (Bannon, 1974). They tend to occur nights or weekends when criminal activity and traffic responsibilities also invoke their greatest organizational demands. Even apart from the other factors noted above, it is not surprising that recurrent spouse abuse calls would receive a lower response priority in such circumstances, at least absent knowledge of past violence or imminent threats to a potential victim's life.

However, this view has been challenged as yet another unsubstantiated assumption. Ford (1990) stated that in his annual review of police dispatches in Indianapolis, domestic calls constituted only 5% of the runs. Therefore, the conclusion that domestic violence assistance provides excessive demands for police service may simply be erroneous and serves as a convenient rationale for avoidance of or screening out of such calls.

4

The Police-Citizen Encounter

SCREENING OUT DOMESTIC VIOLENCE CASES

An important, and possibly unique feature of the police response is that the majority of incidents never reach the criminal justice system. It has long been known that victims and, to a lesser extent, bystanders have both let marital status influence their decision as to whether to call the police (Berk, Berk, Newton, & Loseke, 1984). Embarrassment, inability to make a call without alerting the offender, and previous negative experiences with the criminal justice system all contribute to victim reluctance to report incidents to police. One estimate, underestimated, is that only 2% of domestic violence cases are ever reported by victims to the police (Dobash & Dobash, 1979).

Differential Screening by Victims

In addition to the obvious problem attendant with the police not being called by most victims, differential rates of victim screening contribute to police and public misconceptions that domestic violence is solely a crime of the lower classes. This notion is false. The primary reason why police see far more domestic violence in the poor rather than the middle or upper classes is that the poor tend disproportionately to call the police.

This pattern has long been known to researchers (Parnas, 1967; Westley, 1970). Patterns of economic dependency among "housewives" and a more hierarchical distribution of power in middle/upper class families predict low rates of calling the police. Black (1980) reported that a

> middle class white woman is more likely than a lower class black woman to live in a condition of dependency. . . . She is more likely to live on the earnings of her husband, in a dwelling financed by him . . . "a housewife." . . . Such a woman is not readily able to leave her situation one day and replace it with an equivalent the next. . . . Frederick Engels long ago pointed to the relationship between "male supremacy" and the control of wealth by men: "In the great majority of cases today, at least in the possessing classes, the husband is obliged to earn a living and support his family, and that in itself gives him a position of

supremacy without any need for special legal titles and privileges. Within the family he is the bourgeois, and the wife represents the proletariat" (1884, p. 137). It is therefore almost inconceivable that a totally dependent woman would ask the police to remove her husband from his own house. If he beats her, she is unlikely to invoke the law . . . middle class people are unlikely to call the police about their domestic problems. (p. 125)

Similarly, it has been shown that people prefer to bring their intimate problems to "social equals." As police are seen not to be the social equals of the middle or upper classes, these groups disproportionately shun police involvement in favor of clergy or physicians.

In sharp contrast, lower class black women are generally considered to be the more economically independent from their partner than any group in the United States (Black, 1980). Since lower class black males are not as likely to make as much money as their partner and are proportionally more likely to be unemployed, black women can more easily maintain a degree of independence that allows them the freedom of calling the police when abused.

Further, due to differences in the degree of hierarchy in family structures, many women from certain ethnic groups, even if not middle class, tend not to call the police with their problems. Hence, Appalachian Whites, Asian Americans, Puerto Rican Americans, and so forth have higher rates of victim screening than blacks, again contributing to the misconception of the criminal justice system that domestic violence is disproportionately a problem of lower class black America (Black, 1976, 1980; Parnas, 1978).

Differential Screening by Witnesses

As a result of victim screening, calls from non-participants, or "bystand-ers," have become the primary method by which the criminal justice system is made aware of domestic violence. They are less affected by victim/offender marital status and therefore more willing to call. Bystanders' motivations may, however, provide their own differential screening. Their calls are not necessarily motivated by the seriousness of the assault, but rather the disrup-tion of their own activities due to noise, property damage, or even morbid curiosity.

The significance of witnesses and bystanders in reporting acts of domestic assault may also increase the conception of the problem being concentrated among the lower socioeconomic classes. Due to urban congestion in poor neighborhoods, such cases are more visible to neighbors, more likely to receive their attention, and therefore, be the source of a subsequent call to the police.

For whatever reason, police disproportionately see indigents. As a result, both they and the public tend to view domestic violence as a problem of blacks and the lower classes in general. This conception makes the problem easier to ignore as is done to many "social pathologies" of the poor. If the public realized the extent to which all social classes are affected, a more rigorous police response might be demanded.

The net effect is that the most severe cases of domestic assault may not necessarily be the ones to reach the police. Instead, those most disruptive to public order and thereby known to others outside the family are disproportionately reported (Berk et al., 1984). For this reason, disclosure rates do not appear to be closely related to incident severity. As has been suggested by Pierce (1990), the most severe cases are likely to result in demands for medical assistance, not necessarily the police. In fact, in one early study, Walker (1979) estimated that less than 10% of cases were reported when serious injury resulted.

The dependence upon bystanders to report domestic violence crimes has contributed to the exceptionally low total rates of incident reporting. Estimates of the total rate of disclosure include a 1980 Department of Justice study where 55% of domestic violence cases were never reported to the police (McLeod, 1983). Similarly, in the National Crime Survey reported by the Bureau of Justice Statistics in 1986, only 52% of all incidents of domestic violence discovered in the survey were reported to the police by any source.

Police Screening of Family Violence Calls

In addition to the disproportionate failure of victims and bystanders to report domestic violence, "call screening" by dispatchers has dramatically reduced the incidence of police responses to such calls. In order to maximize allocation of scarce resources and to avoid increasing responses, most modern police departments have routinized call screening. Call screening allows the department to assign priorities to all incoming calls requesting police service. Those with low priorities, usually including simple assaults, will not receive authorization for the dispatch of a police unit until time becomes available. Martin (1979) has also observed that at times call screening has operated to effectively eliminate some categories of calls as well as prioritizing others. This is especially true during peak periods of demands for service, such as weekends and nights, when domestic violence calls are most likely, and responses to these calls may be eliminated altogether (Bannon, 1974).

Call screening should be considered as an adaptive organizational response to help overworked organizations limit environmental demands, being functionally similar to triage in a medical setting. Decisions concerning the immediate dispatch of a unit are primarily predicated upon the dispatcher's long distance determination that commission of a felony is imminent. In responding to ambiguous and volatile domestic violence calls, there is the obvious issue of the agency's well-known antipathy toward these calls coupled with the inherent problems of a stranger not at the scene making a needs assessment. Further, civilians are frequently used as dispatchers in an attempt to conserve money. All too often, the consequence is that untrained and/or inexperienced individuals are screening the calls.

Individual case studies have suggested that call screening has greatly limited reaction of the police to domestic violence cases. Pierce et al. (1984) observed that 50% of the 3.2 million total calls for police assistance in Boston were for service calls, including approximately 80,000 for "family troubles." However, police dispatchers reported an additional 24,400 calls that could have been included in that category but were reclassified by the police. The impact of call screening has also been cited in other studies. For example, Ford (1983) reported that in Marian County, Indiana, between two-thirds and three-quarters of all domestic violence calls were "solved" without dispatchers.

Call screening clearly has serious ramifications. The failure of a department to respond or a delay in the dispatch of an officer may be so long that the emergency nature of a call becomes lost, the threatened violence has already occurred, or the offender has left the scene (Ford, 1983). Victims often receive no attention from police officers that might have prevented new injuries or officially documented past criminal activity. Further, the failure to respond to complaints denies the woman her status as a victim, discouraging her from reporting further abuse, and perhaps encouraging an assailant to believe that his conduct is acceptable.

THE POLICE INTERVENTION

Style of Intervention

Until recently, when police actually intervened, it was rare that a victim or offender, for that matter, would force officers concerned about the task at hand and trained to successfully perform their duties to intervene. Under these circumstances, it is problematic whether any effective intervention would occur when police were actually summoned.

Black (1980) observed four primary styles of response to low-intensity disputes that characterized most domestic violence calls: therapeutic, penal, compensatory, and conciliatory. The *therapeutic* style of crisis management attempts to identify and solve the underlying problems leading to the act of domestic violence. The *penal* style defines a "violator of a prohibition" as one who "deserves condemnation or punishment." A *compensatory* style seeks to redress from an offender to the victim for the harm suffered by the victim. A *conciliatory* style simply defines the deviant behavior as "one side of a social conflict that needs to be settled without regard to who is right or wrong" (Black, 1976).

Bayley (1986) has criticized Black's typology as overly simplistic. He believes that the officer's behavior varies by actions occurring at contact, processing, or exit. Further, when behavior at the termination of an incident is actually examined, he found it difficult to neatly categorize officers into such well-defined categories. Although we subsequently used the categories as a convenient typology, it must be acknowledged that the typology stereotypes a complex behavioral interaction.

Although the police ostensibly have only been given the power to enforce penal sanctions—consistent with the penal style of intervention—this form of intervention is not usually appropriate for most situations of low-intensity interpersonal conflict. A more complex repertoire of responses has necessarily evolved. For situations of verbal altercation, low-level violence, or threats thereof, the therapeutic style is probably the most likely to prevent the escalation of violence by reducing or on occasion eliminating the sources of situational stress. In contrast, the compensatory and punitive styles are perhaps best reserved for cases when the officer encounters repetitive violence where earlier "therapeutic" interventions were unsuccessful, or where the severity of injury or weapons used indicates that severe personal injury has, or is likely, to occur.

Regardless of disputes over terminology, most evidence is that officers do not predominantly adopt either "therapeutic" or "compensatory" styles, the two most effective available intervention techniques (Bayley, 1986). It appears that most officers have instead tended to employ the less effective "conciliatory" style when responding to domestic violence incidents. Black (1980) noted that in his estimate approximately 70% of officers used a conciliatory style, 26% penal, and only 4% used a therapeutic or preventative style to respond to domestic assaults.

Choice of this style may, of course, be dictated by the officer's desire to diffuse the immediate crisis so that he can rapidly leave (Ferraro, 1989a). Of course, the conciliatory style was often combined with the penal style where the officer tried to find a solution satisfactory to both parties, but also noted that the aggressor was to blame and could be arrested.

Intervention style does not appear to be primarily based upon the victim's desires or the severity of her injuries, unless so severe as to literally force the police to use their penal powers. Instead, the choice of police intervention styles has tended to be dominated by situational characteristics independent of severity of the incidents. For example, Black, in his classic study of the police response to interpersonal disputes, found that police: (1) used penal sanctions more toward blacks than whites, (2) were more "conciliatory" and "therapeutic" in orientation toward the middle class compared to the poor, (3) were more conciliatory to adults and more penal toward juveniles, and (4) when threatened or accorded less respect, police rapidly became more penal and coercive in nature (Black, 1976, 1980).

Conciliation appears to be an application of a behavioral model that is applied in many different settings. Skolnick, in his classic work, *Justice Without Trial* (1975), observed that police usually do seek to restore the "semblance" of order rather than trying to "extract, label and process" the offender and resolve the situation permanently. This activity then becomes the "preferred outcome." Davis (1983) has in essence termed the conciliation model to be *containment* defined as a working policy of non-arrest and "order restoration." Order restoration virtually requires adoption of the conciliation approach to prevent the need for arrest.

Does Police Response Vary with the Relationship of the Parties?

In a finding directly relevant to domestic violence disputes, Black reported that the degree of social intimacy of the parties was highly correlated with the police response. He reported that the conciliatory style of control was used for 70% of disputes for married or common-law couples, compared to only 39% for estranged couples and 36% for friends or acquaintances. Conversely, a penal style was used in only 26% of married couple disputes compared to 45% and 57%, respectively, for the other two groups. This was true even though in Black's sample, violence occurred in 60% of the incidents involving married couples compared to only 29% for estranged couples and 14% for friends and acquaintances (Black, 1980). These figures clearly indicate police unwillingness to judge the propriety of conduct among intimates to nearly the same degree as those less closely related.

It is also noteworthy that the acquiescence of police to victim preferences appeared to vary inversely with the strength of the relationships among the parties. Black reported that the police complied with victim preferences in only 37% of the cases involving married or common-law couples compared to 64% for estranged couples. Most of the variance occurred when a married victim requested penal action and the police refused.

Although Black's sample was conducted in the mid-1960s and hence may be more reflective of the "classic" police response before new statutes were enacted, it does support what we believe is often the preferential response of most police toward domestic violence cases. In short, the action that the police will favor if not forced by their commanders or outside pressure (including fear of litigation) will be a passive form of conciliation. The study also supports the continued police tendency to be more punitive toward those groups that lack social power relative to the middle classes. In short, there remains a greater likelihood of the police acting punitively toward the poor and blacks and conversely, a far greater chance that they will be conciliatory and refuse to be "punitive" or make arrests if the victim and offender are white or from the middle or upper classes.

The importance of understanding intervention style is that the officer's actions appear to be determined primarily by ascriptive factors of the victim and offender and by his individual goals, that is, extrication from an unpleasant and (to him) unproductive task, or by organizational standard operating procedures. They are therefore not situationally driven to obtain the outcome most appropriate to the matter at hand. For this reason, police officers have been characterized as having an appropriately modest goal, to obtain a "situational" semblance of order *without* any long-term assistance to the couple or a reduction of violence (Davis, 1983; Ferraro, 1989a).

Information Transmitted by Police

It has been a logical corollary to the officers preferred style of domestic violence case management that little, if any, effective victim assistance information is volunteered. Transmitting information, after all, does not assist the officer's goal to end the immediate crisis or accomplish the minimal mission of restoring "public order." By adopting this extremely shortsighted and egocentric frame of reference, it can readily be seen that a referral may, at best, be irrelevant to the officer and, at worst, lead to further demands for time needed for a prosecution or assistance to shelter personnel to protect the victim. In fact, it has been graphically stated that in most cases, "Victims are confronted with reluctant civil servants whose interests in avoiding the situations outweighed their concern for the victim, an attitude reflected in the quality of information, if any, volunteered on how to prosecute" (Ford, 1983, p. 466).

As a result, Oppenlander (1982) reported that police officers actually give the victim referrals to other agencies in less than 4% of domestic disputes to which they respond, despite the claim by more than 90% of officers in his sample that they knew of such agencies and more than 50% of this group stating that they did make referrals "regularly."

The quality of information supplied is also inadequate. It has been argued that even when information on available shelters or counseling services is offered, such service may not be given to resolve the victim's problems, but may be yet another arrest avoidance mechanism to deter a woman from demanding an arrest (Bell, 1984). For this reason, much of the information given by police on prosecution is incomplete and/or inaccurate. They have often misled women by stating nonexistent procedural hurdles that "prevent" a prosecution or give advice that "this is really a civil matter" even when there is probable cause to believe that all requisite elements of a crime were committed by a suspect. When it is self-evident that a crime has been committed, the information is frequently conveyed in a slanted manner, for example, "You *may* have the right to put him in jail, but think of the economic hardship" (Ford, 1983).

Not surprisingly, recommendations to counseling agents by officers are quite infrequent, and choice of preferred counselors is suspect. For example, in one study of a model program, a special mental health team was available for calls on weekends. The police themselves acknowledged that the group did a good job and was a valuable resource. Despite this, referrals were made in only 2 out of 69 cases (Ferraro, 1989b).

USE OF ARREST POWERS

The Bias Against Arrest

Normally, the primary coercive sanction available to police is an arrest. Since this power is predicated upon the officer's belief that probable cause exists that a particular suspect has committed a crime, it might be assumed that legal variables, such as the strength of the case, are predominate in the decision to arrest. However, at least in domestic violence cases, it is apparent that there is a persistent, if not overwhelming, bias against arrest. Within that context, the decision to arrest is problematic, dependent upon victim and offender characteristics, situational determinants, and patterns of decision making that are not consistent among individual officers nor police organizations.

Obviously, in arrest decisions, legal variables, for example, finding probable cause that all elements of a crime have occurred, are prerequisite to all but the abusive use of arrest powers. However, unlike many other offenses, the perpetrator and location of a domestic assault is known, injuries are obvious, and at least one witness, the victim, is usually available.

If one were to view the arrest situation solely as the result of finding probable cause, a high arrest rate could be surmised. This is not supported. Instead, it has long been established that there is a persistent bias against the use of arrest in such cases. In fact, the closer the relationship between the offender and victim, the less likely it is that an arrest will occur (Black, 1980; Bell, 1984).

It appears that in the decision to arrest, the degree of actual violence or threat of violence to the victim is often only of minimal significance. Even when victims were in danger and requested an arrest, most studies have reported that officers have consistently refused to make arrests (Black, 1980; Brown, 1984; Burke & Loseke, 1980-1981; Buzawa, 1990; Davis, 1983; Parnas, 1967). Empirical measurements of the rate of arrests have varied depending upon the definition of the crime and officer estimates of the existence of necessary elements of a crime. However, regardless of measurement techniques, arrests have clearly been infrequent with estimates of 3% (Langley & Levy, 1977); 4% (Lawrenz, Lembo, & Schade, 1988); 7.5% (Holmes & Bibel, 1988); 10% (Roy, 1977); and 13.9% (Bayley, 1986).

Most researchers have also observed that the use of arrest powers has primarily been reserved to cases of disrespect or challenges to police authority. Most actual arrests were when the officer actually witnessed the assault. Although this may be attributable to excessive caution, it is equally likely that the arrest was due to the continuation of aggression rather than the event that brought the officer to the residence. Such behavior may be interpreted as a threat to the officer's authority, a factor that has often been cited in general police literature as a reason why arrests occur (Berk et al., 1984; Black, 1980; Davis, 1983; Ferraro, 1989b; Harris, 1973; Manning, 1977; Skolnick, 1966).

Ford (1987) stated it was also probable that officers were more inclined to arrest when they believed a subsequent disturbance would result that required another police response, rather than basing their arrest decisions upon severity of or concern for the victim's welfare. Empirical research substantiates this theory. One recent study showed that only 16% of offenders were arrested even when the victim was injured. Of the 33% of a sample that were repeat calls, there was no difference in the rate of arrest. This demonstrated that arrest policies toward recidivists remained the same as for new offenders (Buzawa, 1990).

Other studies have noted that officers set preconditions to the use of arrest powers that were clearly not mandated by statutory authority. For example, in one study, 58% of the officers stated that they would make an arrest only in the case of a serious injury. This clearly is not a requirement for a misdemeanor arrest. Laws and policies state that the seriousness of an injury, if relevant at all, should only determine whether the offender is to be charged with a felony or a misdemeanor.

The bias against arrest is not confined merely to the United States. Although most of the research published has analyzed United States' arrest practices, a growing number of international studies have confirmed similar results. For example, in one Canadian city, London, Ontario, prior to a new mandatory arrest policy, the police charged domestic violence assailants with assault in only 3% of the cases that they encountered despite victim injuries sufficient to have them advise the victim to seek medical attention approximately 20% of the time (Burris & Jaffe, 1983). Similarly, studies in Great Britain (Freeman, 1980; Hanmer, Radford, & Stanko, 1989); the Netherlands (Zoomer, 1989); Australia (Hatty, 1989); and Northern Ireland (Boyle, 1980) have criticized the police refusal to make arrests in domestic violence cases. For a summary of such literature, see Stanko (1989).

The Decision to Arrest: Situational Factors

Despite the heavy bias against arrests, it is still worth considering the conditions under which an arrest will occur. This shows not only where arrests are predicted, but also provides insight as to when new policies favoring arrests are most likely to meet resistance.

Victim Preferences

In all but mandatory arrest jurisdictions, an informal, but real, operational requirement for an arrest is that the victim desire the officer make an arrest. Without victim concurrence, most jurisdictions have policies that actively discourage arrest (Bell, 1984). Empirical studies have confirmed that the probability of an arrest increased by 25 to 30% if the woman agreed to sign a complaint and decreased by a similar amount if she refused. Berk and Loseke (1980-1981), and Worden and Pollitz (1984) stated that victim preferences accounted for the largest variance in arrest rates in every study that they examined.

Given the police desire to obtain "good" arrests resulting in convictions, the importance of this factor is obvious. Officers know that without victim cooperation, any charge will either be dismissed by the prosecutor or result in an acquittal for failure of evidence. They may also believe that if the victim is unwilling to extend the effort to initiate a complaint, the seriousness of the injury may not warrant disrupting their own schedules.

In contrast, due to the overwhelming organizational bias against arrest, some studies have reported that victim preferences or injuries are of limited importance in the decision to arrest. These decisions instead are far more influenced by organizational factors. For example, Bayley (1986) reported that assailant arrest was not even correlated with victim wishes. Further, in a recent study sampling Massachusetts police departments, the police could not have been strongly affected by victim preferences because they were unable to even report the victim's arrest preferences in more than 75% of the cases (Buzawa, 1990).

Police Responses to the Victim's Life-style

Although the officer's deferral to the victim's expressed wishes might be appropriate, other less benign typologies of the victim also influence arrest rates. It has long been known that police make far fewer arrests in cases where the victims are married and living with the offenders (Dobash & Dobash, 1979; Martin, 1976; Worden & Pollitz, 1984). While this claim has been disputed in at least one study, Berk and Loseke (1980), the consensus is that the relational distance between the offender and the victim does indeed affect the probability of an arrest. The rationale appears to be that when police perceive a commitment to a relationship between the victim and offender, this lessens the likelihood of the victim ultimately cooperating with the police and prosecutors to secure a conviction, a factor of great import to the police (Black, 1976).

Although it is now unusual to have anyone forthrightly express the belief, it is also possible that some officers may still believe it legitimate for a husband to physically chastise his wife "with moderation." However, even if one adopts this regressive perspective, the "right" may not extend to boyfriends or casual acquaintances. In fact, the probable real effect of this attitude is at the largely unconscious margins of the arrest decision. From the officer's perspective, if not the victim's, a particular case may be marginal in nature, being relatively weak or involving less severe conduct.

The second victim-orientated criterion is the officer's subjective percep-tion that violence may be a "normal way of life" for a particular victim and offender (Black, 1980). As discussed by Ferraro (1989b), when officers observe a regularly recurring pattern of violence, they believe it is part of the social fabric of a couple's lives. Consequently, they are less likely to believe that any police response, including an arrest, will be successful in deterring future violence. In this regard, they dichotomize between "normal citizens," similar to themselves, and "deviants," perhaps seen to use excessive alcohol, not speak English, belong to minority groups, or be in an interracial marriage. For this group, battering is perceived by many officers as merely a part of overall family pathology and not amenable to any intervention (Ferraro, 1989b).

Various authors have also noted that police have responded with less of a service orientation to blacks and other minorities. They are therefore less likely to use arrest powers in cases of domestic assault for these groups (Black, 1980; Stanko, 1989). Of course, it is possible that the assumption that officers react directly to race and ethnicity is an insufficient analysis of a complex phenomenon. Ferraro (1989b) instead has reported that the key variable appears to be the typology of the victim as belonging to a deviant population group. This may partially be based upon the victim's race.

Patterns of differential enforcement for different racial groups may also diminish as the cadre of nontraditional officers in a department increases. For example, one study in the Detroit Police Department has found that black and female officers presented different operational arrest patterns than those of white males, the subjects of traditional analysis (Buzawa, 1990). This distinction, which will be discussed later, may become more important as the number of nontraditional officers increases.

Police Evaluation of Victim Conduct

Police officers often view victims through the prism of their own beliefs as to the appropriateness of their conduct. A necessary component of their job is to make rapid value judgments in circumstances where reality is not clear. In the face of ambiguous facts, research on police responses to rape, sexual assault, and domestic violence all indicate that officers make judgments based upon their inherent assumptions regarding proper victim conduct (Manning, 1978; Skolnick, 1975).

Because the nature of the relationship is viewed as a valid factor in evaluating criminal activity, officers have scrutinized the victim's behavior as well as that of the assailant. Typically neither is judged to be guilt free (Stanko, 1989). In this context, the victim's demeanor toward the officer may be as significant as her degree of injury. If she is rational, nondemanding, and deferential toward the police, her story may evoke more sympathy and attention, probably because it is assumed that within the context of the relationship the woman had retained those same characteristics (Ford, 1983; Pepinsky, 1976).

In contrast, if the woman is abusive, disorderly, or drunk, the officers rarely make arrests or, at least, fail to follow victim preferences. For example, after conducting extensive field observations in Detroit, it was noted that when officers did not follow preferences of female victims, it was often because she was not "liked" by the responding officers who would label her as being too "aggressive," "obnoxious," or otherwise causing problems to the officer (Buzawa, 1990).

Several subsets of the officers' critical examination of victims' conduct have been evaluated. For example, police have been said to accept moderate violence as a legitimate response to marital infidelity (Saunders & Size, 1986). Similarly, the desires of male victims of domestic assault, even when severely injured, have not been accorded high value by the police. In Detroit, it was found that with few exceptions, the female victims were not dissatisfied with the police response to a domestic assault. However, none of the male victims were satisfied with how the incident was handled (Buzawa, 1990).

In fact, it has been already well documented that male victims are less likely to report a domestic assault (Langley & Levy, 1977; McLeod, 1984; Steinmetz, 1980; Straus, 1977-1978). It is possible that a contributing factor to their reluctance to report assaults is a realistic expectation of limited police understanding. Officers may incorrectly assume that a male victim should be capable of preventing violence by a woman. When he doesn't, he no longer conforms to accepted standards, and the decision to arrest his partner is rarely made. Unfortunately, we cannot determine if this is a solid critique. Although significant research attention has been focused on the impact of traditional male views upon the police treatment of female victims, similar research has not yet been extended to encompass the effect of the traditional views of "proper conduct" as an influence upon the police response to male victims.

Assailant Demeanor and the Decision to Arrest

Assailant demeanor and other situational characteristics of the police-citizen encounter present a further source of variance in the arrest decision. It has long been known that an arrest nearly always occurs if an assailant remains violent in the officer's presence (Ferraro, 1989a). Perhaps because of the implied threat to the officer's authority or a lack of respect, an arrest is likely if the offender is perceived to constitute a direct threat to the officer independent of the strength of the case (Dolan, Hendricks, & Meagher, 1986). Similarly, when police respond to gang locations or other places where they feel threatened, they tend to act more aggressively and use their powers far more frequently (Ferraro, 1989a).

Also, it has been observed that arrests are quite likely when the suspected abuser is belligerent or drunk. Bayley (1986) found that two-thirds of offenders who were hostile were arrested, whereas *none* that were civil toward the police were arrested. Buzawa (1990) also noted that victim injury was not as predictive of arrest as offender demeanor. For example, in one case, an uninjured "victim" that had called the police cut the assailant with a butcher knife near his eye requiring several stitches. No arrest was made because the assailant was drunk, and in fact the officers were not sure if he could have been potentially dangerous to the victim.

Who Initiated the Contact?

Another "extralegal" factor apparently affecting the decision to arrest is who initiated the police citizen encounter. One would normally expect the police to be more responsive if the victim initiated the call. This should indicate her commitment to stopping the conduct and thus increase their likelihood of a response. However, findings suggest the reverse. Berk and Loseke (1980-1981) found that when the victim alerted the police, as opposed to a third party, the probability of an arrest declined 21%. This finding was not corroborated by Worden and Pollitz (1984). If it is later confirmed, it is possible that when a bystander has become involved to the extent of calling the police, the conflict may no longer be perceived by the police as confined to principals, but has become a matter concerning the maintenance of public order. Another possible explanation is that when a bystander calls, the initial police characterization of the call would be as a "disorderly conduct" or a "disturbance." The initial characterization of the call might effect how the call is processed. In addition, the police statistics may not be sophisticated enough to allow all the types of possible charges that might result from a domestic assault. Therefore, the call from the spouse may be more likely to be classified as a domestic assault than a call from another citizen. As noted earlier, the touchstone of police intervention in domestic violence cases has been whether or not such activities constituted a *public* disturbance versus a private dispute. Intervention for the sake of victim protection has not often been the primary determinant of police arrest decisions.

The Decision to Arrest: Organizational Factors

Another set of critical variables impacting upon the arrest decision relates to organizational and officer characteristics. There are known to be major differences in the propensity of different officers to arrest abusive intimates. For this reason, many studies have concluded that the police-citizen encounter is profoundly unpredictable from the viewpoint of the victim and offender. The response depends heavily upon the officer's orientation toward domestic violence, skill level, and time constraints. Although difficult to quantify or predict, they are evident in practice. For example, when the intervention occurs at the end of the officer's shift, an arrest is less likely because the crime is not considered worthy enough to justify the officer staying late (Berk & Loseke, 1980-1981; Ferraro 1989b; Stanko, 1989; Worden & Pollitz, 1984). Still other studies have focused upon unrelated attributes of the criminal justice system to determine if they have impacted upon arrest rates. Conditions such as overcrowded jails or lockups do appear to reduce domestic violence arrest rates (Dolan et al., 1986), as do inconvenient court hours or court locations (Ford, 1990).

Profound differences also exist within particular police departments and among different agencies. Within a department, it appears that both attitudinal factors and demographic variables add to such variance among officers.

Attitudes of Officers

Individual attitudes of officers toward domestic violence cases appear to dramatically effect arrest preferences. When confronted with a report of serious injury to a victim, one study found that approximately 50% of the officers would regularly arrest, whereas the remaining 50% would not arrest on any consistent basis (Waaland & Keeley, 1985).

The reasons for this difference are not clear. It is acknowledged that officers often have different role expectations. Some see their mission as being a crime fighter or maintaining public order; others tend to be more service oriented, concerned with assisting victims. From this, one might expect that those oriented toward a service approach would make arrests at a higher rate than those adopting a crime-fighting style. Although this may be of some help in determining which offenders are arrested, the overall rates of arrest for both groups appear to be equally low, consistent with the bias against using arrest powers. One study has reported that service-oriented officers had an approximately 10% arrest rate compared to 8.5% for crime fighters. Hardly an overwhelming difference (Worden & Pollitz, 1984).

Sociodemographic Characteristics of Officers

Differences in the use of arrest powers have also been attributed to the demographic characteristics of officers. Distinctions between male/female officers have most frequently been examined in this regard. The preponderance of research suggests that female officers, although not necessarily more likely to arrest, are reported by victims as being more understanding, showing more concern, and providing more information about legal rights and shelters. In one survey, 40% of a sample of male and female officers stated that the two groups handled domestic violence situations differently. Male officers perceived female officers as "softer," "more uncertain," "weaker," "more passive," "slower," and "lazier" while female officers saw themselves as "feminine," "nonviolent," and "passive" (Homant & Kennedy, 1984). Also, many of the female officers had a self-image of being more concerned with domestic violence than male officers (Homant & Kennedy, 1985). The extent of a male/female dichotomy has been questioned by several authors (Ferraro, 1989a; Radford, 1989; Stanko, 1989) who believe that to work in a male-dominated organization, female officers behave similarly to men because of occupational socialization or simply to fit in. This theory is still generally unproven by empirical research, indeed, research has tentatively supported the existence of attitudinal and behavioral differences between the two groups.

Other officer demographic features have been considered to effect arrest rate and the overall response of officers. For example, Buzawa (1990) has found that age of the officer effects response. This result was consistent even when controlling for exposure to the training program. In the same study, it was also found that black officers arrested for such crimes more frequently than whites. Although the reason for this distinction is uncertain, it is consistent with Black's theory that when conduct is viewed as normal in the context of victim/offender behavior patterns, arrests are not made. Black officers may not share the same stereotypes regarding "normal" behavior in black families as do white officers. Also, as Black (1980) has noted, black officers often display even more coercive behavior toward black citizenry than their white cohorts.

Profound differences in arrest rates and other attributes of performance have also been found between different police departments. This is not altogether surprising. It would be expected that arrest rates should increase in departments with extensive domestic violence training emphasizing a proactive approach, and where policies require an increased role of arrest.

Jurisdictions where a "mandatory arrest" or presumptive arrest policy is in effect should, at least in theory, have higher levels of arrest. However, in addition to the impact of express policy, there may be differences among departments based upon more generalized departmental attitudes, such as orientation toward service calls and characteristics of their community. Although there is little empirical research in the context of departmental responses to domestic violence, a number of researchers have noted generalized performance differences in service versus law enforcement oriented agencies.

Similarly, the characteristics of a department's service community have been shown to affect police practices. For example, in one study, suburban departments had the highest reported rates of domestic violence, perhaps because suburbanites tended to report complaints to police. However, the police initiated criminal complaints at a rate lower than rural and urban departments. Bell (1984) concluded that the three different types of departments—urban, rural, and suburban—had markedly different policy orientations toward domestic violence.

DOES POLICE INTERVENTION HELP?

The View that it Worsens Abuse

Early empirical research in the 1970s and research of feminist scholars to the present maintain that because police attitudes were hostile and skill levels poor, their intervention would have little positive or even a negative impact upon a violent family. The earliest empirical research, Bannon (1974), observed that the police had been to houses where a felonious assault had occurred five or more times in 50% of the cases and at least one time in 85% of the cases. Consequent research analyzing repeat calls to addresses of homicide and assault participants confirmed that police had previously responded to approximately 90% of homicide addresses (Breedlove, Sandker, Kennish, & Sawtell, 1977; Victim Services Agency, 1988). Such figures may, to a certain extent, exaggerate the percentage of repeat calls due to family turnover in low-income housing and assaults among or to other family members. However, the logical conclusion was that inadequate police response either failed to prevent future violence or perhaps even "encouraged" recidivism.

This premise assumed that when officers perfunctorily intervene and give ineffectual or inappropriate advice to victims to "get a warrant" or warn the couple not to disturb the peace, the abuser will lose concern over criminal justice sanctions and even feel reinforced about the normalcy of his conduct. Conversely, the victim might believe that society offers no recourse and tacitly condones the conduct.

This is supported by Hanmer, Radford, & Stanko (1989), who noted, "If the police don't offer unconditional protection to women, they are in fact condoning the violence" (p. 6; see also Ford, 1988; Straus, 1980). Finally, a poor intervention may increase the risk that the offender will retaliate against the victim, if the victim called or even, in a warped sense of justice, if the victim's screams, indirectly caused the offender the embarrassment of a police encounter.

The Police May Help

The results of recent empirical research, however, suggest a different, more complicated pattern. Those victims that called the police may not have felt that the police performed poorly. Other studies have reported that battered women rate the effectiveness of police services quite low (Binney, Harkell, & Nixon, 1989; Bowker, 1982; Pahl, 1985; Roy, 1977). Unfortunately, as noted by Elliott (1989), these studies were small, samples were non-representative, and did not differentiate between types of service provided. In addition, such studies did not distinguish between police behavior before and after recent trends toward more aggressive policies.

To determine whether the police have had a positive impact, it is appropriate to see if victim goals are being met. In one study, 52% of domestic violence incidents were brought to police attention. The primary goal of a plurality (37%) of these women was the prevention of future assaults rather than rehabilitation via arrest and conviction for current criminal activity. Of married women who did not call the police, 41% were subsequently assaulted within a six-month period. In contrast, of those who did call, only 15% were reassaulted (Langan & Innes, 1986). Intervention, however imperfect, may therefore have accounted for a 62% decline in rates of reassault among married women and a less significant, but still major, reduction of 41% of all women, including spouses, former spouses, and singles. Similarly, a large-scale National Crime Survey study based on 128,000 interviews suggested that calling the police was associated with reduced risks of reported violence and, further, that there was no evidence that violence escalated as a result of intervention (Langan & Innes, 1986).

As discussed earlier, an inappropriate police intervention might have the deleterious effect of increasing the severity of the subsequent assaults due to retaliation or increased frustration. Langan and Innes (1986), however, found no such result. In fact, they reported a reverse statistical correlation wherein 2.9% of the women who called the police had a subsequent incident more serious than the first, compared to 4.5% of the women who did not call the police, translating into an apparent 36% improvement upon intervention.

ARE WE IN A POSITION TO EVALUATE THE EFFECT OF THE POLICE?

Clearly, the actual impact of police intervention is complex and requires additional research. Previous research examined victims whose problems have received police attention. As previously noted, a majority of victims do not call the police. Perhaps the most insidious effect of past poor police practices may be a contribution to the inordinately high rates of victims not calling the police or victim screening. Therefore, a critical examination needs to be made of those who do *not* make calls to determine if a significant percentage are deterred because of their past experiences, or the "common knowledge" of police victim interaction. In addition, it cannot automatically be assumed that merely because a plurality of female victims view prevention of future violence as the primary goal of police intervention, that this should be the goal of intervention. A crime has typically been committed, and traumatized individuals may focus solely upon preventing future pain without considering other relevant issues. Finally, if any type of police intervention leads to lower rates of recidivism, a more effective disciplined police intervention process could, and should in theory, prevent even more future violence.

5

Judicial Response to Domestic Violence

The victim's problems with the criminal justice system have not ended with the police. In fact, she may find when by luck and persistence, she overcomes police indifference she may reach a judicial system with problems just as severe as with the police. In fact, many of the problematic characteristics of the police-victim encounters are repeated in the context of the courts.

THE ORGANIZATIONAL CONTEXT OF COURT ACTION

To understand how victims and offenders are treated by the judicial system, it is necessary to first examine the organizational context in which courts handle domestic violence cases and the problems attendant with the "classic" judicial response to domestic violence.

Civil versus Criminal Forums

Domestic violence cases may be heard by either specialized civil courts or criminal court. A victim usually can choose in which forum to proceed. A citizen's criminal complaint can be filed for assault, battery, intentional infliction of emotional distress, or violation of the terms of a temporary restraining order if available. A victim also may ask a prosecutor to initiate a criminal action. Alternately, she can file a complaint for actionable civil injuries. The orientation of these courts is markedly different. Civil courts provide the victim with the advantage of being oriented to resolving individual disputes, compensating victims for injuries, and deciding the custody of legal incompetents such as minors. Furthermore, there is no concept of "prosecutorial discretion" whereby an officer of the criminal court can decline to prosecute a case. Finally, cases in such tribunals are decided on the basis of a preponderance of the evidence, a factor that favors finding misconduct in disputant cases.

Despite this, most domestic violence cases are still heard in criminal courts. Exceptions are for specific actions for temporary restraining orders, protective orders, and cases appropriate to specialized family and divorce courts. Due to general case overload, most civil actions take an exceptionally long time to hear, often in excess of five years in major urban areas. Hence, they often become irrelevant and are of little assistance to domestic disputants. Further, most civil actions necessitate the retention of legal counsel, which is costly and requires considerable victim initiative.

Even the nature of available civil remedies tends to favor selection of a criminal court. With the exception of the quasi-criminal injunctive orders to be later discussed, most civil remedies transfer assets from an offending to an aggrieved party. This is simply not appropriate for most cases of spousal violence, particularly if divorce proceedings are not contemplated. Finally, despite their record of giving questionable advice, police are typically the primary referral source for victims entering into the judicial system. They are trained to recognize criminal conduct and may either arrest a suspected offender, thereby initiating a criminal case, or advise the victim to fill out a criminal complaint. This has the effect of directing victims toward a criminal forum.

The Victim's Experience in Court

When a victim enters a prosecutor's officer, she is confronted with an organization with its own often arcane goals and operational norms. She may gradually learn that the primary intent of the criminal courts is to enforce *society's* rights to sanction activities harmful to the public order, and thereby punish offenders and deter future misconduct. Such powers are an exceptional imposition upon the rights of the citizenry. The courts therefore require proof beyond a reasonable doubt of the defendant's commission of a crime. Finally, judges and, to a lesser extent, prosecutors, tend to be process oriented and acutely aware of the police officer's limited authority and the defendant's constitutional rights.

Because the court's primary goals are societal in nature, victims do not have the right to insist upon prosecution. The decision as to whether to charge, which charges to advance, and which charges to later dismiss or settle, does not require the victim's consent. The foregoing may appear to be intuitively obvious. However, it is doubtful that most victims understand the nature of the criminal court organization, and tend erroneously to assume that the prosecutorial staff operates primarily to redress their particular grievances.

The second major organizational characteristic of the criminal court enforcement of domestic violence laws is the marked distinction in treatment accorded misdemeanor and felony crimes. Although most domestic violence is classified as a misdemeanor, the distinction is yet another product of the relatively low esteem given such cases and perhaps a reflection of the inherent sexism of the criminal justice system. Certainly in most other contexts, the offender's conduct would otherwise be termed a felony. For example, in one recent National Crime Survey, it was reported that more than one-third of misdemeanor domestic violence cases would have been termed rape, robbery, or aggravated assault, all felonies, if committed by strangers. In 42% of the *remaining* misdemeanor cases, an injury occurred. This rate of injury for a misdemeanor crime was higher than the combined injury rate of all of the foregoing felonies (Langan & Innes, 1986).

These surprising statistics occur primarily because in American jurisprudence, the mere presence of the injury is not usually determinative of the severity of the crime charged. Unless a homicide occurs, evidence of premeditation and use of a weapon are given far more importance in the charging decision. Because domestic violence events are typically treated in isolation, the existence of a persistent pattern of battering a spouse or other family members usually does not constitute evidence of intent.

Alternately, such crimes may be downplayed simply because they are crimes against women, a disfavored group. Regardless of the reason, the effect of the dichotomy is to lessen the importance of a court "wasting" its scarce resources to process domestic violence cases (Langan & Innes, 1986).

THE JUDICIAL BIAS AGAINST "RELATIONSHIP" CASES

There exists a well-documented general bias against "relationship" cases where the offender and victim know each other and have some right to interact with the other party (Stanko, 1982). This dislike is particularly due to time constraints and the high proportion of such cases in the system. The Vera Institute (1977) estimated that in more than 50% of all violent crime felonies and one-third of combined violent and property crimes, the victim and the offender were acquainted. Such cases are over represented because they tend to be comparatively easy for the victim to report and the police to apprehend the proper suspect.

These cases are known to trouble courts. Although a common problem in a civil setting, the complexity of a relationship often negates the simplistic right/wrong dichotomy needed to convict in a criminal tribunal. Court personnel tend to believe that defendants in a relationship case may be influenced by the relationship itself. Thus, they are perceived as not being a "hard case" and much less likely to be recidivistic than those responsible for violence, property loss, theft against strangers, or drug addicts who are unable to stop their criminal activity (Smith, 1983). Finally, "relationship" cases may be denigrated because they do less violence to the "public" order and appear to be a personal problem thereby belonging, if anywhere, in a civil court.

With sufficient resources, the general court bias against relationship cases, and domestic violence cases in particular, would be an interesting but not overly significant example of judicial behavior. Unfortunately, this is not the case. The current overriding organizational characteristic of federal and state courts is the crisis of excessive caseloads. The present drug crisis and resultant budgetary pressures dominate the attention of state and federal judiciary. Some recent estimates are that as high as 65% of all criminal cases are drug related. State courts handle 95% of such cases (Labaton, 1989).

The devastation of the tide of drug cases has, in turn, been compounded by the longer sentences imposed by courts and new federal and state sentencing guidelines removing considerable discretion in judicial sentencing. An unexpected consequence of such legislation has been that applicable defendants have virtually no incentive to plea bargain as their sentences cannot be substantively reduced.

A report of the Conference of Chief Judges of the nine most populous states commented that lawmakers and officials who had adopted such policies failed to consider the impact of the huge flood of cases on the courts. Conferees warned of either an imminent or existing caseload crisis and possible breakdown of the system if solutions were not found soon (Labaton, 1989). In the state court system, the family courts were considered to suffer the most. For example, in the past three years, New York State family court filings increased by 699% and in 1989 accounted for up to 532,000 cases annually. Many such cases are for juvenile drug-related crimes or for custody of children whose parents are incarcerated or are considered incompetent for drug-related reasons. Because of the impact on children, these cases take considerable court resources. Because the total number of judges has not markedly increased (in New York City's family court, no increase at all since 1983) the average caseload and court backlog is growing tremendously (Labaton, 1989).

Under this kind of pressure, it is not surprising that prosecutors, judges, and their staffs attempt any possible means to informally reduce caseloads by diversion from the criminal justice docket or outright dismissal. Because domestic violence cases are usually misdemeanors, which have never been favored, or if felonies are first offenses, they are not usually encompassed by

sentencing guidelines. It is not surprising that they become disproportionately subject to pressure for settlement or dismissal.

In Minneapolis, the head of the criminal division of the Minneapolis City
Attorney's Office analogized its mandatory arrest policy to a funnel. More
cases were being given by the police to the prosecution who had no additional
staffing. The net result was that these cases competed for the same limited
amount of judicial and prosecutorial time. This forced the agencies to
informally drop cases (Balos & Trotzky, 1988).

CASE ATTRITION BY VICTIMS

Domestic violence victim attrition/case dismissal rates are extraordinarily
high. This may occur either by the victim dropping charges or her refusal to
appear as a witness. A series of studies in different jurisdictions published by
the Center for Women's Policy Studies has consistently shown that absent
unusually aggressive measures, attrition rates for victim-initiated cases hover
between 60% and 80% (Lerman, 1981). Similar confirmatory accounts have
been reported (Cannavale & Falcon, 1986; Field & Field, 1973; Ford, 1983;
Parnas, 1970; Williams, 1976; The Vera Institute, 1977).

The reasons for such high rates of attrition are varied. *First*, the attitudes
of the prosecution and staff tend to influence victims to drop the charges.
Unlike most "non-relationship" cases, court personnel in domestic violence
cases make victims feel personally responsible for case outcome. In the
former context, the victim is considered to have suffered a direct harm.
However, the public order is also deemed to be harmed. For this reason,
prosecutors encourage or may even require by subpoena the victim in a
non-relationship case to support any resultant prosecution by appearing as a
witness.

In domestic violence incidents, the violation to the "public order" is not
as evident to the prosecutorial staff. This has naturally led to their profound
ambivalence about intervening in private disputes. Not unexpectedly, they
subtly or even at times, overtly, encourage the victim to drop the charges.
For more detailed accounts of this process, see Bannon (1975) and Smith
(1979, 1983).

Second, victims sustain high perceived and real costs to continue prosecution. Although available evidence does not support the belief that most, or
even a significant percentage of, victims are subject to subsequent retaliation
or intimidation by the offender to drop charges, isolated cases where a suspect
has murdered a victim and/or court personnel have occurred. While statistically an unlikely occurrence, no one can provide certainty to an often terrified
victim. In many judicial systems there is an utter failure to give victims

information about methods to protect themselves via temporary or permanent restraining orders.

Although less dramatic, there is also the real possibility that indirect economic harm of a continued prosecution may deter a victim from continuing a charge. If the victim continues to cohabitate with the offender, she may fear the possibility of direct loss of income on the household should he lose his job. In other cases, a reduction in alimony or child support may be a source of concern. Such loss may in fact occur in the event of a conviction or if extensive court time is required.

Direct economic harm to the victim may also result if she is required to take time from her own job and arrange for child care to support a prosecution by making court appearances. In many cases, she is forced to wait for hours to give a few minutes of testimony, or as often happens, to have her time be totally wasted when the case is continued to a later date.

Third, the victim's attitude toward the crime and the offender alter over time. Memories of the crime and the perpetrated harm recede after an extended period. The cyclic nature of battering may result in a prolonged "honeymoon," where the offender seeks to make up with the victim due to atonement or fear of prosecution. In time, continued prosecution of the case may become the only event that reminds her of the "bad times" and threatens to end the current harmonious period.

Fourth, many victims, whether or not accurately, may tend to attribute part of the causation of the violent incident to their own conduct. Self-doubt and guilt are even more significant than for other victims of violent crime, and may uneasily coexist with the victim's desires for retribution, deterrence, and perhaps rehabilitation that led the victim to charge the offender. Feminists would, of course, note that such a result is predictable given the constant pressure of a sexist society.

Fifth, the complex motives of victims are predictive of relatively high "drop-out" rates. Ford and Burke (1987) list five predominant motives for prosecution: (1) curiosity over what the system might do; (2) confirmation of her status as a victim (a sort of "coming out" as a battered woman); (3) a promised increase in her own legitimacy as a victim in subsequent police encounters; (4) a matter of principle, that is, a crime has been committed and should be reported; and (5) revenge for the crime (but not usually extending to a desire for imprisonment of the offender).

Curiosity might appear to be an unusual motive for the decision to charge a crime. In this context, the legal system, commencing with the initial police intervention, often provides little substantive information suggesting options until charges are actually filed. Given the known desire of the criminal justice bureaucracy to get rid of these "undesirable" cases, one might cynically observe that information on alternatives to prosecution is provided *not* with the intent to arrest the offender, but because the victim becomes a nuisance in bureaucratic terms by refusing to leave the system without prodding. If researchers do not wish to merely become advocates of prosecution for its own sake, one must understand that these reasons are reflective of reality. Many domestic violence victims simply are not as deeply committed to continued prosecution as are other victims of criminal behavior.

Ford (1984) suggests that prosecution may be the only available alternative for many women to gain control in a relationship. The actual prosecution is of secondary importance to the control gained as a "power resource" through threats. Thus, the criminal justice system is used as a strategic tool of the victim rather than for its expected outcome.

CASE SCREENING BY COURT PERSONNEL

Explicit Screening of Cases

Regardless of the reasons for the attrition rate among domestic violence victims, their failure to assist the prosecutorial process has served to reinforce frustration and cynicism among court professionals. These bureaucrats simply lack the time, background, or inclination to understand why victims drop charges. They often express comments such as "No real harm must have occurred," "The victim was never serious about the charges," The victim was a "masochist" for continuing to live with the man, and the victim had "lied earlier to the police to obtain revenge on an unrelated dispute" or to influence a pending divorce, custody, or child support proceedings, and was now "scared she would be caught in a lie." Even the more sympathetic court personnel believe that the victim is "trapped and has now realized that the criminal justice system can't help."

In the context of the overwhelming lack of resources in the court bureaucracies, the high victim dropout rate reinforces prosecutorial decisions to exercise their discretion by refusing to bring or later to dismiss charges. One result has been that both victims and offenders are faced with a judicial system that appears to have little predictability. Cases that would be continued in another context are dropped despite clear evidence that would otherwise sustain a prosecution.

How are Cases Differentially Treated by Prosecutors?

The tendency of prosecution to use a number of "extra legal" variables to differentially screen cases has often been noted (Ellis, 1984; Schmidt & Steury, 1989; Stanko, 1982).

Victim Motivation

Perhaps of greatest significance is the acknowledgment that prosecutors believe they should evaluate victim motivation and assess her commitment to continued prosecution. This is considered a legitimate case discriminator independent of the inherent strength of the case. In a position that was otherwise favorable to the goals of increased involvement in domestic violence cases, the National Association of District Attorneys (NADA) stated that in considering whether to prosecute, a district attorney *should* consider if it is "likely" for a victim to cooperate, if the victim agreed to live apart from the defendant, and in general, "the relationship of the parties" (NADA, 1980).

Inherent in this position is the assumption that a commitment to continue prosecution is a valid case discriminator. The authors instead suggest that this factor is profoundly incorrect as a basis for the exercise of prosecutorial discretion. If there nominally is primary concern for the injuries suffered by the victim and the prevention of future violence, the bureaucratic goal of achieving a high rate of convictions should be subordinated.

Despite this belief, the reality has been that concern for the victim's misfortune has not usually been the prime motivator of the actions of the prosecutors. Instead, the critical factors have been whether the injury was of a type and quality that could not be ignored, for example, death or an overwhelmingly vicious and publicized attack, or if the victim "stubbornly" refused to quietly go away and had the resources or influence to force a decision to prosecute. The prosecutor's office was then forced to confront a complaint. If the charge was filed and abandoned, measurements of their capability to obtain high conviction rates was adversely affected. The possibility that the victim may have achieved her goals in the interim would, of course, be irrelevant in this context. Hence, even a "successful" prosecution from the viewpoint of the victim would be viewed as an organizational failure if dropped.

Victims Continued Relationship with the Offender

As a result of this attitude, one study found that the victim's continuing relationship with the offender has been a key factor in decisions of whether to continue or drop prosecution (Schmidt & Steury, 1989). They reported that charges were far more likely to be filed if the victim claimed to have no continuing sexual intimacy with the offender. Hence, although they contradicted earlier research by finding little effect of marital status per se, they found a significant negative correlation between prosecution and victim/offender cohabitation. This result could be attributed to organizational concerns over victim's commitment to prosecution, or more charitably, to a victim-oriented concern that maintaining a prosecution in this context might prove dangerous to the victim.

Offender Characteristics

An important factor in deciding to prosecute has been whether the prosecutor perceived that the offender is truly recalcitrant or unlikely to be recidivistic. As expected, a history of prior abuse is not strongly related with future charging decisions. Of perhaps greater surprise is that the prior record appears to influence the prosecutor even more than the evidentiary strength of the case (Schmidt & Steury, 1989). Also, for many offenses, use of drugs and/or alcohol has been taken by officials to "mitigate" the intent and therefore the nature of a crime. In domestic violence cases, the reverse appears to be true in the context of offender sentencing (Schmidt & Steury, 1989). Although this may be a result of a generalized phenomenon of "tougher" law enforcement against substance abusers, it may also be due to the prosecutor's recognition that drug-induced violence is likely to reoccur at higher rates than among non-addicts.

Organizational Factors

Finally, organizational imperatives beyond the knowledge or control of most victims affect the decision to initiate or continue prosecution. Perhaps the most significant of these is the tendency of prosecutors to treat police-initiated arrests more seriously than complaints of victimization filed by citizens. This is understandable. Police and prosecutors need their mutual support. Prosecution legitimizes officer arrests while police give prosecutors evidence that sustains high conviction rates.

If a police officer arrests a suspect and the prosecutor declines to pursue a charge, there is an implicit challenge to this compact. The police officer may be personally affronted or interpret this decision as questioning his competency. Also, police-initiated charges might be viewed by the attorney as somehow having been screened for content by his decision to make an arrest.

Whatever the reason, such charges are typically considered to be more "legitimate" (Cole, 1984; Jacoby, 1980; Schmidt & Steury, 1989). In contrast, citizen-initiated complaints are treated as having no organizational sponsor with no designated bureaucrat having responsibility or accountability for any decisions.

Imposing Procedural Barriers to Prosecution

Even if the prosecutor's office does not formally dismiss the charges and thereby officially take responsibility for dropping a case, a variety of barriers have been erected to prevent the charge from being filed, or if filed, subsequently pursued. For example, in one large county in Indiana, a major obstacle was placed before domestic violence related arrest warrants issued on a victim's behalf. In normal nondomestic violence cases, an arrest warrant was apparently issued within one to two days of the victim filing a complaint. This did happen when a domestic violence complainant was accompanied by an officer, thereby showing the prosecutor that the officer had a personal attachment to the matter, and demonstrating the officer's appraisal of the case's legitimacy. However, when the complaint was initiated solely by the victim's actions, it took two weeks or longer to issue a warrant. Also, after this two-week period, often a warrant for arrest would not be issued at all. Instead, a summons to appear in court would be *mailed* to an offender instead of the issuance of an arrest warrant. As a result, in only one-third of the cases was any arrest made within one month after a victim initiated a complaint, and in only 62% of cases after six months (Ford, 1983). Obviously, the prosecutor's office was neither trying to process such complaints nor were the police eager to effect service of warrants.

Other procedural hurdles have been used to screen out "undesirable" or "frivolous" cases. In the same Indiana county studied by Ford, a mandatory three-day waiting period existed before a domestic violence complaint would be received by the court. This forced a second victim-initiated action prior to any organizational evaluation of the merits of the case (Ford, 1983). This particular procedural hurdle is virtually unheard of outside of domestic violence complaint processing. The net effect was to force the victim to reaffirm what may have been a very traumatic initial decision to prosecute before there was evidence that the prosecutor's office would help.

Not surprisingly, this served as an effective mechanism for discarding domestic violence complaints. Ford noted that 33% of married women filing domestic violence complaints had these placed on hold and 78% of them did not return. This compared to corresponding figures of 60% and 52%, respectively, for those who had filed for divorce, and 46% and 59% of those who actually divorced. In this case, the screening device ostensibly used for organizational reasons to eliminate "frivolous" domestic violence complaints effectively omitted approximately two-thirds of these women who had already called the police and then taken the further initiative of filing a criminal complaint, already a small minority of abused victims.

It is apparent that a complex interaction has evolved between the motives and actions of the domestic violence victim and the prosecutor's office. Each profoundly misunderstands the other's individual and organizational motives and needs. Victims of most crimes assume that once criminal justice processing is commenced, the procedure is straightforward. Few realize the inherent complexities created by the need for their continued involvement or the uncertainty caused by the requirements of protecting the offender's constitutional rights. Unfulfilled expectations, normal to most victims, are coupled with the domestic violence victim's often ambiguous or conflicting motives for prosecution, and the apathy and even hostility of a bureaucracy nominally dedicated to protecting his or her interests. Under such circumstances, it would be unrealistic to assume anything other than high rates of victim attrition.

Similarly, the prosecutor and his staff often cannot understand why victims refuse to leave abusive partners and/or fail to rigorously assist prosecution of their abusers. This misunderstanding in turn affects their behavior in a manner that reinforces these misperceptions; that is, even more women drop charges or fail to appear because of the indifference or cynicism of court personnel or the erection of Byzantine barriers that "test" her commitment to prosecute. Subsequent victim actions reinforce negative staff attitudes. Low rates of prosecution and conviction in turn reinforce and justify the persistent reluctance of police officers to become involved in domestic violence cases. Thus, two negative feedback loops are strengthened by the initial victim/prosecutor misperceptions.

ACTIONS BY THE JUDICIARY

Cases that are not filtered out of the system by action or inaction of the police, victims, or prosecutors often receive summary dispositions by the judiciary.

Although it would be easy to overgeneralize, judges appear to have shared the consensus of prosecutors that most domestic violence cases could not readily be helped by the full prosecution of an offender (Dobash & Dobash, 1979; Field & Field, 1973). Given the organizational context of extreme time pressures and limited resources, it is not surprising that it has been repeatedly noted that judges have minimized domestic violence cases, and disproportionately acted to dismiss them (Parnas, 1970, 1973).

Similarly, the sentencing of convicted domestic violence offenders has, at least until recently, been seen to be quite lenient with few offenders being required to spend time in jail (Parnas, 1973). One study was made in Ohio of all misdemeanor domestic violence assault charges in the state during 1980. This research was conducted *after* Ohio passed a new domestic violence statute that was enacted to sensitize the criminal justice system to the problems of battered women. Although termed misdemeanors, many of these cases involved injuries and potentially serious conduct, which in another context would have been termed to be felonies. The sentences imposed graphically illustrated how the crimes were minimized by the judicial system. Of the 1,408 cases, 1,142 or 81% were dismissed. Of the

1,142 dismissed cases, 1,062 or 93% were dismissed because the victim requested this action or failed to appear in court. Of the remaining 256 cases, 166 guilty verdicts or pleas were received. Despite being in a jurisdiction noted for harsh sentencing, only 60 miscreants or 36% spent any time in jail with one-third spending between 1 and 15 days (including time spent in jail awaiting trial), one-third between 16 and 30 days, and only one-third more than 20 days. Similarly, only 12% of the miscreants were fined more than $100. Simple probation, instead of imprisonment or fines, was the sentence in almost two-thirds of the cases (Quarm & Schwartz, 1983).

The effect of such judicial attitudes cascades throughout the criminal justice system. The judiciary retains the potential of leading the criminal justice system by example or direction. After all, they are the ultimate authority having the power to ratify or condemn the actions of the police and prosecutors, as well as defining the parameters and seriousness of a particular crime. They may use such power to compel effective action or, as in the past, strongly imply that domestic violence it not a "real crime." At a minimum, police policies that emphasized the role of arrest have been undermined when such cases are routinely dismissed or the sentencing reflects the judges' disparaging attitudes.

PART II

The Process of Change

6

The Impetus for Change

The modern movement for change in the police response to domestic violence arose from an unusual confluence of political and legal pressure from women's rights and battered women advocates, legal research, and organizational concerns over the possibility of liability if the police continued past practices of neglecting domestic violence victims.

FEMINIST AND POLITICAL PRESSURE ON THE CRIMINAL JUSTICE SYSTEM

Political pressure began to mount in the late 1960s and early 1970s over the perceived inadequacies of the criminal justice responses to issues of interest to women. The women's rights and feminist movements that began to emerge in the early 1970s raised consciousness about societal neglect toward the unique problems of women. The inability of the criminal justice system to respond to violence against women was initially focused on rape and stranger assaults. Soon, however, concerns broadened, and women's rights activists began to recognize the severity of the problem of violence in the home.

The movement to assist battered women through shelters sprang from hundreds if not thousands of local community-based volunteer efforts. These quickly acquired the services of paid and volunteer attorneys, "victim advocates," and social workers. These trained professionals rapidly realized that the needs of domestic violence victims were not being met by criminal justice agencies.

The cavalier attitude of male-dominated police agencies and prosecutor offices to such crimes was quickly discerned. Concerns rapidly mounted when advocates began to realize that police appeared to arrest everyone *but* domestic violence assailants (Berk & Loseke, 1980). As a result, police recommendations advocating more aggressive use of arrest became the natural "consensus" among battered women activists. (Neimann, 1987, quoted in Ferraro, 1989b). This group has provided the leadership for promoting the enactment of state and federal statutes. This occurred at the national level, largely unsuccessfully, and at the state and local levels, where an unprecedented success was achieved, at least on paper.

Societal pressures toward a more "law enforcement" oriented attitude to domestic violence also became significant. Although a possible over-generalization, the past decade has been a period marked with the increased societal propensity to use its coercive powers to "solve" social problems. As might be expected, the threats of random violence and drug abuse are generally seen by the public as a "law enforcement" issue. These justify increasingly punitive sentences and are not considered amenable to careful studies of causation, prevention, and offender rehabilitation. Placed in this context, it is not surprising that spouse abuse became a law enforcement issue.

There are parallels in this regard with the initiation of the earlier reform era of the late 1880s. However, distinctions between the current and earlier periods can be noted. With today's mass media, national feminist organizations, with the growing ability to influence special interest lobbyists who influence legislation, the movement to greater law enforcement has become a national rather than a regional phenomenon. Finally, the existence of support services to assist women with shelter and legal advocacy, even if not well funded, has given increasing visibility to large numbers of injured women. This has continued to reinforce the necessity of effective police action.

For example, the recent spectacular revelations in Boston, Massachusetts, of Carol and Charles Stuart's murder/suicide have properly been recognized as being reflective of the prevalence of domestic violence and the inability of police to recognize or effectively confront such issues.

RESEARCH AS AN AGENT OF CHANGE

Seminal Research in the 1960s and 1970s

Research linking the criminal justice system to domestic violence has had a dramatic effect alerting policy elites to the existence of the problems of domestic violence, and "legitimizing" and reducing modifying support for certain policies. In this regard, the research itself becomes a factor independent of the adequacy of the design, accuracy of the conclusions, or the utility of the particular policy nostrums being promulgated.

Academic interest in family violence began with concerns over child abuse. The seminal article, "The Battered Child Syndrome" in *The Journal*

of the American Medical Association by Kemp, Silverman, Steele, Droegenmuller, & Silver (1962) focused on the necessity of physicians and other
primary caregivers such as social workers to recognize and intervene in such
cases. This article and subsequent publications, however, focused less on
criminal law implications and more on the etiology of the problem and
treatment of the victim and offender (Pleck, 1989).

Several years after the Kempe article, Parnas (1967) published, "The
Police Response to the Domestic Disturbance" in the *Wisconsin Law Review*.
This article was followed in 1971 by one in a more widely subscribed journal,
"Police Discretion and Diversion of Incidents of Intra-Family Violence"
published in *Law and Contemporary Problems*. These studies graphically
demonstrated that the police response to domestic violence was perfunctory.
Shortly thereafter, Morton Bard wrote, *Family Crisis Intervention: From
Concept to Implementation*, in 1973. This study analyzed the effect of a Law
Enforcement Assistance Administration (L.E.A.A.) demonstration project on
family crisis intervention. This project, in turn, became the theoretical
foundation for many other family crisis intervention projects (Liebman &
Schwartz, 1973).

Although the specific uses of family crisis intervention will be covered
later, the impact of the Bard study was that it focused attention on the concept
that changes in the police response could dramatically affect future violence
and decrease injuries and other costs to police departments.

Louis Mayo, the former Division Director for the National Institute of
Justice, stated that he believes Morton Bard deserves credit for drawing
national attention to the police response to cases of domestic assault. In 1967,
Bard had approached the former United States Law Enforcement Assistance
Administration (L.E.A.A.), suggesting that it was unaware of a major social
problem. While the national policy at that time was for police to do as little
as possible and then leave the situation, Bard convinced them that crisis
intervention techniques would have a significant potential for improvement.
He was able to have the Office for Law Enforcement Assistance fund a
feasibility study for a special unit of officers.

The final "classic study" was by Marie Wilt and James Bannon (1977),
entitled *Domestic Violence and the Police: Studies in Detroit and Kansas
City,* published by the Police Foundation. They demonstrated that domestic
violence was directly related to homicide, that police were repeatedly called
to the scene of most domestic violence related homicides, and therefore,
ineffective police response "contributed" to the excessive rates of death and
injury to victims and the high costs of intervention to police departments.

The cumulative impact of the foregoing literature and consequent studies
was to assist development of a research consensus that police response to
domestic violence did not conform to the reasonable expectation of proactive

policing, that inappropriate or passive police responses did contribute to the high social costs of domestic violence, and finally that alternate methods of providing police service could reduce the heavy toll of domestic violence.

The Minneapolis Experiment

More recently, one widely publicized study by Lawrence W. Sherman and Richard A. Berk, in Minneapolis, "The Specific Deterrent Effects of Arrest for Domestic Assault" (1984), has had an enormous impact. It clearly galvanized the movement toward increasing reliance by the police upon the use of arrest powers. This research was initially funded due to the interest of the National Institute of Justice (NIJ) to fund general deterrence research. This issue arose out of a National Academy of Sciences Report, entitled *Deterrence and Incapacitation: Estimating the Effects of Criminal Sanctions on Crime Rates*, edited by Blumstein, Cohen, and Nagin (1978).

The Minneapolis study was a limited experimental design that did not purport to definitely answer or even necessarily address the question of the "proper" police response to domestic violence. However, despite initial disclaimers to the contrary, the Sherman and Berk study immediately became by far the most cited study in the area. Joel Garner of NIJ credits Sherman for making the topic of family violence a focal point of their agency. The subsequent funding of additional research on that topic is directly attributable to his Minneapolis study (Garner, 1990; Garner & Visher, 1988).

This research received wide publicity for several reasons. First, it concerned several areas of media interest: domestic violence, a topic of growing saliency in the early 1980s, and poor performance of police, always of interest.

Second, the conclusions were desired by most feminists and battered women advocates. For years, they had advocated without much effect that police should treat the crime of domestic violence far more seriously and with respect for victims. Therefore, to some extent, the attention placed on the study was fortuitous, and it supported an idea favored by a significant policy elite. Under such conditions, research disclaimers were likely to be ignored.

Third, at least one of the authors, Lawrence Sherman, had and continues to espouse the belief that "social scientists should generally view publicity seeking as a duty rather than a vice" (Sherman, 1986, cited in Sherman & Cohn, 1989). He recounts, "decisions made about how to manage the story," including persuading local television to feature documentaries that later provided such "action" tapes, for national news shows (even before the results of the experiment were known). Efforts to continue to manage the press continued even to the extent of releasing the final results during the

Sunday before Memorial Day as it would then "face less competition on a slow news day" (Sherman & Cohn, 1989), and notifying the *MacNeil Lehrer Newshour* of the study's release well in advance. Such publicity efforts, extraordinary for social science research, were justified as an attempt to "get the attention of key audiences affecting police department policies" (Sherman & Cohn, 1989, p. 121). As Sherman remarked, he also "wanted the audiences to be influenced by the recommendations and be more willing to control replications and random experiments in general" (Sherman & Cohn, 1989, p. 122).

It is also possible that the massive publicity campaign was designed to pressure an ambivalent federal funding agency (NIJ) to replicate the study in additional cities instead of using its scarce resources to study different aspects of the police response to domestic violence. In any event, NIJ decided to replicate the Minneapolis study in six cities and adopted the same experimental design, a source of controversy among researchers. According to Joel Garner, arguments against that specific design were "not particularly persuasive," and a "replication" meant employing the same methodology (Garner, 1990).

The impact of the study was certainly partially due to the extreme publicity it received and the impression that its conclusions, however tentative, were federally funded and supported. Under such conditions, administrative debates on the relative merits of arrest compared to other reforms then being attempted were clearly made more problematic. Finally, despite its acknowledged limitations, the study has reinforced to the point of orthodoxy the view among feminists that police should use arrest powers and a mandatory arrest policy should be instituted.

The research implications of Sherman and Cohen's work clearly deserves further study. A very interesting dialogue between proponents and opponents of such research was recently published in several articles (Binder & Meeker, 1988; Sherman & Cohn, 1989). This was the topic of a widely attended debate at the 1990 Academy of Criminal Justice Sciences Annual Meeting in Denver.

Two positions acknowledge that widely reported research, although preliminary in nature, may dramatically affect social policy. As might be expected, the differences are in the perception of the responsibility of researchers. Binder would appear to prefer to wait for final research prior to publicizing preliminary findings. In contrast Sherman perceived that he has a normative duty to try to affect change in the response to a critical problem. He believes this despite knowledge of research limitations and the concern of others that prematurely basing policy on a preliminary study that is extensively publicized might cause adoption of "an innovation that does more harm than good" (Lempert, 1987).

LEGAL LIABILITY AS AN AGENT FOR CHANGE

The third major force changing the police response to domestic violence has been the growing administrative realization that failure to respond exposes individual officers and police departments as organizations to substantive risks of liability awards, fines, and injunctions. This has dramatically curtailed their freedom to operate on a "business as usual" basis.

It has generally been recognized that the seminal case forcing police change has been *Tracey Thurman et al. v. the City of Torrington, Connecticut* 595 F. Supp. 1521 (Dist. Conn., 1984). Because of its graphic portrayal of police indifference and its profound impact on police procedures, it is worthwhile to discuss Thurman in detail.

In this case, Ms. Thurman and other relatives had repeatedly called the police, pleading for help from her estranged husband, but had received virtually no assistance, even after he was convicted and placed on probation for damage to her property. When she asked the police to arrest him for making threats to shoot her and her son while still on probation from the earlier incident, they told her to return three weeks later and get a restraining order in the interim. This, of course, was not a legal requirement for action. In any event, she did obtain the court order but the police then refused to arrest her husband citing a holiday weekend. After the weekend, police continued to refuse to assist based on the "fact" that the only officer that could arrest him was on vacation, an obvious delaying tactic. In one chilling final rampage by her husband following a delayed response to a call for emergency police assistance, Thurman was attacked by her estranged husband and suffered multiple stab wounds to the chest and neck, resulting in paralysis below her neck and permanent disfigurement.

Her attorneys argued two major theories of police liability since adopted in virtually all subsequent cases. The first is based on a claim of negligence. Simplified, it states that police, being sworn to protect the citizenry, have a duty when requested to take reasonable action to prevent subsequent victim injury from a known offender.

The second theory used in the Thurman case was that the police violated the constitutional rights of Ms. Thurman by failing to provide her with the equal protection of the law guaranteed by the 14th Amendment to the U.S. Constitution. The claim was based upon the differential treatment accorded to a man who batters his spouse versus an assault by a stranger. Since most victims of spouse abuse are women, this was seen as a problem of sex discrimination. Issues of sex discrimination are, in turn, settled on the basis of whether the classification is substantially related to an important government objective.

The court found that a clear hidden agenda of the police department existed. It held that police actions appeared to be deliberate indifference to complaints of married women in general, and Thurman in particular. This conduct constituted negligence and violated the equal protection of the law guaranteed Thurman by the Constitution. A $2.3 million verdict was awarded to Ms. Thurman and her son. An excellent description of the legal rationale of the judgment is contained in Eppler (1986).

The Thurman case was widely reported in the popular press and in academic journals. It graphically confirmed the extreme financial penalty that could be imposed on police departments when they abjectly fail to perform their duties. In addition, it confirmed that in appropriate cases, these massive liability awards would be upheld.

The impact of *Thurman* and similar cases was twofold. Fear of future liability awards became a prime factor motivating departmental administration, out of self-protection at least, to begin to require more paper work to justify its actions. In some cases, this proved a major reason for departments to adopt administrative policies favoring a presumption of arrest. Fear of liability awards was even more of an impetus to those jurisdictions that had adopted by statute or department policy a mandatory or presumptive arrest. Such statutes could easily be used by plaintiffs' attorneys to establish the standard of care that police owed to victims of domestic violence. In this context, it is noteworthy that one state's mandatory arrest law has already been cited in a legal advocacy journal as providing a "sound basis" for asserting a legally enforceable right of action to victims hurt by the police failure to make arrests (Gundle, 1986; restated in Victim Services Agency, 1988).

The second major impact was the proliferation of consent decrees resulting from negotiated settlements of class action lawsuits that alleged a past policy of police to not make domestic violence related arrests. At various times, the police departments in New York City; Oakland, California; and Dallas, Texas, have all operated under consent decrees requiring them to treat domestic violence as a crime, to make arrests where appropriate without consideration of marital status in the arrest decision, and to advise the victim of her legal rights.

The importance of these orders is that if the order is violated, a clear standard of care has been set—and not met—making a liability suit relatively easy to prove as the standard. Finally, if the violation was intentional, the police administrators and/or the officers in question risk contempt of court sanctions, including jail in extreme cases. For a summary of such cases, see Ferraro (1989a) and Victim Services Agency (1988). Unfortunately, while such consent decrees have been imposed in a number of jurisdictions, no known research has empirically examined the extent to which actual operational practices may have changed after such an order was placed into effect.

As noted by Stanko (1989), the key to these factors is that by the late 1970s and early 1980s, there was a highly unusual blend of research, pressure from feminist advocates, and an administrative "need" for change. These factors all operated in one direction—to change the police response to domestic violence and increase arrest rates.

THE ABORTED FEDERAL RESPONSE

The initial tactic of advocates of change was to publicize the failures of the criminal justice system and obtain a federal commitment to force structural change. Sympathetic Congressmen in the late 1970s and early 1980s held numerous hearings on proposed federal legislation focusing primarily on shelter funding and mass education and training for affected agencies. See especially Domestic Violence and Legislation with Respect to Domestic Violence: Hearings in Senate 2759 before the Subcommittee on Child Resources and Human Development of the Senate Committee on Human Resources, 95th Congress 2nd Session (1978), and hearings in the Senate 1843 the Domestic Violence Prevention and Services Act, 1980; Hearings on Senate 1843 before the Senate Committee on Labor and Human Resources 96th Aug 2nd Session 1980.

These hearings uniformly heard witnesses explaining the widespread nature of the problem, decrying the inability of law enforcement and the judiciary to take effective action, and emphasizing the necessity of federal funds to assist in upgrading and standardizing shelters and other victim resources. Ultimately, a widely cited report was issued by the U.S. Commission on Civil Rights, *The Federal Response to Domestic Violence* (1982). In this report, domestic violence was called "a civil rights problem of overwhelming magnitude." Ironically, virtually all of the federally funded programs that were cited in this report as being useful to effect change were eliminated before the report was published. The Law Enforcement Assistance Administration (L.E.A.A.) had funded numerous innovative police programs. Other agencies, such as the Legal Services Corporation, providing direct services to battered women in their dealings with the police and the judiciary, were curtailed.

Despite such attention, and in sharp contrast to federal efforts to stop child abuse, little consistent federal funding has assisted victims. Strong conservative opposition continued to keep federal funding of shelters and research on domestic violence prevention and treatment at a minimum. For an example of such a reaction, see Senator Jesse Helms's critique against providing *any* federal support to domestic violence shelters because they constituted "social engineering," eliminating the husband as the "head of the family" (126 Cong. Rec. 24, 120, 1980).

Several federal agencies such as the Attorney General's Office, the National Institute of Justice, and the Bureau of Justice Statistics have been active in funding much needed research and demonstration projects; however, for the past 10 years, federal funding of large-scale projects has been lacking despite efforts of the former Law Enforcement Assistance Administration or current and past federal funding of child abuse programs. To a large extent, this is due to a generalized problem of available funding in most federal agencies. It also clearly reflects the unwillingness of the federal government to treat domestic violence as a major problem demanding a solution. A notable exception was the U.S. Attorney General's Task Force on Family Violence Report issued in 1984. Unfortunately, like earlier initiatives, funding to implement its recommendations never materialized. However, it did serve as a symbol of federal interest in promoting attention to the issue and a springboard for several funded projects.

Despite the lack of a strong impetus from the federal government, or perhaps due to recognition that this was unlikely in the near future, state governments and individual communities have been forced to address the necessity of change by passage of new statutes and local initiatives. Such efforts at change, almost unprecedented in the area of criminal justice, will be discussed in the next several chapters.

7

Organizational Changes

SPECIALIZED FAMILY VIOLENCE UNITS

As described earlier, the first innovation adopted by police departments was the development of family violence crisis intervention teams. First developed by Morton Bard in New York City under an LEAA grant in 1967, these programs quickly spread. By 1971, at least 14 police departments had crisis intervention training programs, and dozens more had plans to adopt them (Liebman & Schwartz, 1973).

The theory behind such units was that each department would train a cadre of specialized officers in mediation techniques and crisis intervention. Bard had previously employed these tactics in a different setting and believed they had potential for both reducing officer injury as well as reducing violence resulting from police mishandling of conflicts.

Training was done primarily by consulting psychologists using small group training techniques. Bard became the first person employing role playing as a strategy for police training. Further, Bard introduced the concept of tracking domestic calls. Officers maintained file cabinets in their cars with records of each call and case histories. At that point in time, before the advent of computer data bases, this was highly unusual. The concept of such units depended on several critical assumptions: (1) a highly trained cadre of officers could transcend the abysmal performance level of the department in general; (2) once that group was trained, their performance would act as a catalyst for change for other officers; and (3) in most cases, domestic violence was ultimately best treated as a pathology of the family unit, not primarily a crime deserving of punishment.

The officers became generalist-specialists and were not devoted solely to handling disturbance calls. Instead, they performed their regular patrol duties when not covering a domestic call. Of course, to some extent, this was a compromise between the desire for a dedicated trained force and the relative inefficiency of special purpose units. However, a common misperception is that Bard intended to restrict crisis intervention training to specialized units. The initial unit was for purposes of the feasibility study only, and it was possible that the entire department would have subsequently been trained

(Mayo, 1990). Another misconception was that these units never made arrests. Although this was clearly not preferred, arrests were made where "appropriate" (Mayo, 1990).

The only major evaluation of these programs was undertaken by Bard himself. In his final report for LEAA, he found that several "favorable" results occurred: (1) repeat calls to the police increased—reportedly because the victims were satisfied with past police interventions; (2) no officer injuries were sustained in the experimental precinct; (3) a high number of officer referrals were made to social and mental health agencies; and (4) arrests declined. Based on the above, Bard concluded that it appeared that the unit was effective in reducing the rate and severity of domestic violence in the test precinct.

Bard then convinced Mayo, who was then Division Director of NIJ, to select this as the first project for NIJ's Training and Demonstration Programs. The program was then established in 10 cities using local resources and establishing procedures to develop departmental trainers.

The program did recognize the need for the entire department to receive such training as crisis intervention calls were frequent and unpredictable. Further, it was believed that the basic techniques of crisis intervention enhanced all aspects of police performance, particularly with its emphasis on strategies for police safety. Subsequently, the New York City Family Crisis Intervention unit and the follow-up programs received considerable favorable publicity from New York City and its federal sponsor, the project's funding source. It subsequently became a model for numerous other programs (Liebman & Schwartz, 1973).

The proclaimed "success" of Family Crisis units was not without its critics. A highly critical article by Donald Liebman and Jeffrey Schwartz (1974), challenged the basic assumptions of success in the New York City experiment. They noted that available data indicated even more homicides occurred in the experimental precinct, and total levels of domestic violence also apparently increased. Since the decrease in officer injury was itself not statistically significant, the conclusion was that available evidence did not support adopting massive crisis intervention units.

The practice of using crisis intervention teams also had several major operational disadvantages. A primary concern has been that the potential volume of domestic violence cases would far overwhelm available resources unless much higher funding levels for such specialized units were made available. In an era of constant budgetary pressures, any dedicated unit may be criticized as being an inefficient use of scarce resources. Here the costs of training and maintaining specialized units were obviously far greater than a "downscoped" general training program administered to all officers.

Second, officer burnout in other specialized units, such as narcotics and vice, suggests that officer burnout and turnover would be a serious problem over time and lead to a continually high training cost. It required extensive and costly training for a cadre of officers that had relatively high turnover rates. Turnover was high because the officers did not perform "worthwhile" tasks as defined by the police occupational culture or as formally measured by the police department.

Third, many calls are reported to 911 dispatch and ambiguously reported as a family "problem" or another crime altogether. This means that in many cases it would be inappropriate to first send a specialized team. Therefore, some training is necessary for all patrol officers to facilitate the initial police response and ensure subsequent needed cooperation for intervention by the more effective crisis intervention program.

Fourth, even Mayo and other proponents of crisis intervention techniques did not deny there has been some operational disagreement as to whether the police as an institution would ever be capable of handling a "social work" type function implied by such teams.

Finally, while the crisis intervention model might have limited viability in the case of well-trained officers entering low intensity conflicts, the model was inherently easy to corrupt. Many departments gave cursory instructions in crisis intervention by senior patrol officers, not trained psychologists, and then proclaimed that their officers were well trained in "modern" police techniques.

As noted earlier, pressure from feminists and the possibility of adverse legal actions also made "non-punitive" options typified by crisis intervention less attractive. Most feminists have strongly stated that they believe that domestic violence is fundamentally a crime with a victim and a perpetrator, not a conflict situation to be "managed" (Ferraro, 1989). As such, they believed that the conflict resolution model typified by crisis intervention teams did not satisfy victim needs for safety nor protect her legitimate right to seek retribution.

By 1984, the U.S. Attorney General's Task Force on Family Violence strongly suggested that the criminal justice system should take actions consistent with recognition that acts of domestic violence are crimes not "conflict" situations (see also Victim Services Agency, 1988). As the result of such criticism and the failure to receive new federal demonstration project funds, most of the departments that had adopted crisis intervention units ultimately abandoned or severely restricted such units at least in the response to domestic violence.

Few police departments currently rely on dedicated police family crisis intervention teams as the primary method of responding to domestic violence calls. However, variations of this specialized detail continue to be attempted or advocated utilizing police-social worker teams, and specialized teams as backup resources for households that regularly report violent outbursts. Also, despite not being in vogue at the present time, such teams may have set the stage for current reform efforts. While the specific attention placed upon crisis intervention units has waned, Mayo (1990) believed that these programs were effective in sensitizing departments to the issue of responding to domestic violence. In a survey conducted by Bard and NIJ, it was found that more than 50% of the nearly 400 departments attending a nationwide executive training program on crisis intervention said they were actively pursuing increased attention to domestic violence within their agency.

8

The Increased Role of Arrests

After the disillusionment with crisis intervention training by the early 1980s, primary emphasis has been placed upon efforts to deter crime by increasing police use of arrests for highly specific domestic violence charges.

Several major changes in procedural and substantive criminal laws have occurred that demonstrate the increased policy preferences to stress use of arrest powers. Efforts have been made to greatly enhance police *ability* and the *willingness* to make domestic violence arrests.

REMOVAL OF PROCEDURAL BARRIERS TO ARREST

Procedural impediments to the use of arrests have been dramatically curtailed. Prior to the late 1970s, all but 14 states required that an officer witness a misdemeanor prior to making a warrantless arrest. This was in sharp contrast to the ability of an officer to arrest without a warrant upon finding probable cause that a felony had occurred. Since most acts of domestic violence are apt to be classified as simple assault and battery, a misdemeanor, this had been a key limitation. If the act was not repeated in the presence of the officer, no arrest could be made. This victim either had to separately initiate and sign a criminal complaint—actions rarely undertaken by domestic violence victims but still more common than police arrests for battery. Alternately, the police might arrest for a specific non-domestic violence charge such as "disorderly conduct" or "public intoxication." These charges, however, rarely connoted the possibility of a serious assault. They would therefore usually be "flushed" from the system as soon as a magistrate acted.

Starting with the 1977 enactment of Pennsylvania's landmark Protection from Abuse Act, 35 PA Cons. Stat. Ann. sec. 10185 (Purdon, 1977), virtually all states, except Alabama and West Virginia, adopted legislation that allows to some extent a police officer to make warrantless arrests for an unseen domestic violence related misdemeanor assault. These statutes, however, are not uniform and often contain significant exceptions such as short time periods or existence of visible injuries.

EXPANSION OF THE SUBSTANTIVE GROUNDS FOR ARREST

Substantive bases to make arrests were also increasing at the same time procedural restrictions were being swept away. Temporary restraining orders have increasingly been authorized by statutes to place a prior restraint upon those whose prior conduct indicates a proclivity to violence.

Of particular importance to the police, many such statutes expressly provided for enforcement of an order by warrantless arrest, for example, their enforcement was "criminalized" even if no substantive crime had occurred. This was in sharp departure to the older style "peace bonds," where conduct might have been prohibited by a magistrate but enforcement was via forfeiture of the "peace bond." This has considerable potential importance since, in the past, police, acting at times with extraordinary caution, often refused to find that probable cause existed to believe that a misdemeanor assault had been committed by a suspect. Because the TRO/Peace Bond could be used to restrain any contacts between the suspect and the person being protected, police now had a far more flexible vehicle to find probable cause to make a warrantless arrest. The existence and violation of the orders also was much easier to prove in a court. This fact has made a victim lawsuit against the police much easier to prove.

Despite the statutory differences discussed in numerous law review articles, collectively these changes in procedural and substantive laws constituted an almost unprecedented effort to remove archaic restrictions, and encourage police departments to respond to the growing political pressure to use arrests more frequently.

THE INCREASED POLICY PREFERENCE FOR ARRESTS

The Evolution of an Arrest Preference

It has long been known that arresting certain domestic violence offenders was both proper and essential. After all, making an arrest is the only method with which police may ensure the separation of the couple and prevent violence, at least until the offender has been released or has "sobered up." Similarly, despite a strong past bias against arrest, an arrest for non-domestic violence specific charges such as "drunk and disorderly conduct" or "public intoxication" was often used. Although rare arrests for assault and battery itself were made when the injuries to a victim were fatal or so severe they could not be ignored. Finally, even in the past, arrests were a method of the police regaining control from an assailant who was disrespectful or was otherwise threatening to the officer's situational dominance (Bittner, 1967, 1974).

By the early 1980s, the consensus on the historically limited role of arrest had been shattered. It had been replaced by an expanding debate among police administrators, advocates for battered women and their feminist allies, and academicians about the growing practice of using arrest for its alleged deterrent value. Finally, there was a growing realization that other traditional criminal justice measures were inadequate in either preventing or punishing domestic violence offenders.

A new consensus favoring arrest began to emerge in the early 1980s. Crisis intervention techniques began to lose adherents. Deterrence as a general preference for crime control became a dominant perspective in mainstream academic literature and in policy circles. Not surprisingly, the two trends were linked. Deterrence as a justification for use of arrest was increasingly advocated by many researchers and activists (see especially Dobash & Dobash; 1979, Martin, 1976).

The Rationale of Deterrence

Deterrence theory, as applied to arrests of domestic violence offenders, is part of a trend among crime control academicians to stress prevention of future criminal behavior via deterrence rather than rehabilitation. Von Hirsch (1985) noted the shift from a "treatment model" favoring rehabilitation of offenders that had predominated during the 1960s and early 1970s to one that conceded that available treatment had little or no effect. The increased challenge to the treatment model left a void that deterrence theorists could fill. In addition, economists began to apply their disciplines to criminal justice policy development, an area that had been the province of sociologists, psychologists, and political scientists. They theorized that "crime could effectively be reduced . . . through sentencing policies aimed at intimidating potential offenders more efficiently" (Von Hirsch, 1985, p. 7, requoted in Gottfredson & Hirschi, 1988, p. 200).

Gottfredson and Hirschi have noted that deterrence as the preferred response has been replaced by *incapacitation*. Incapacitation is in some ways the ultimate cynical response to crime prevention, which is to remove the criminal from society. However, it has not yet been applied to domestic violence offenders, leaving deterrence as the predominant "fad." Arrest in this context is merely the logical instrument of such a policy.

The concept of deterrence itself can conceptually be subdivided into specific and general deterrence.

Specific Deterrence

The theory of specific deterrence relies on the belief that once an offender is punished by an arrest or other criminal justice sanction, resulting threats of future punishment will be more credible. This increases the fear of further punishment, which, in theory, inhibits further violence (Ford, 1988). The theory rests on several assumptions: (1) being arrested is a punishment distinct from the traditional view of punishment as a sentence after a defendant's guilty verdict or guilty plea; (2) a potential recidivist believes he will be "punished" again should he continue his conduct; and (3) that his conduct is not spontaneous and/or irrational and thereby not able to be easily deterred.

Some researchers have argued that the use of arrest in domestic violence cases fit three criteria. Williams and Hawkins (1989) in a cogent article, note that while classic deterrence theory has focused upon formal punishments, or "the intrinsic consequences of legal sanctions" (Gibbs, 1985; Pasternoster, 1987), this analysis is inadequate. Instead, they argue that in domestic violence cases, it is the act of being publicly labeled "wife beater" and the attendant fear of adverse publicity that may deter potential recidivists. The shock of an arrest, especially to a man who does not often confront the police, might thereby deter future violence.

The application of deterrence theory to arrests in domestic violence is also consistent with some tenets of psychologists who have stated that the best time to attempt to correct deviant behavior is immediately after the act of violence. When this is done, the punishment prevents the tacit reinforcement of such behavior by allowing the improper activities to go unnoticed and unpunished. If, as Williams and Hawkins (1989) believe, the arrest is itself the act of punishment, prospects for deterrence might be enhanced because the punishment would be "administered" almost immediately after the incident, as opposed to waiting months for a slow and inconsistent criminal justice system.

Several preliminary studies have shown that arrests may have some value as a deterrent. As described earlier, a controlled, but limited, experiment was conducted in Minneapolis, Minnesota. The study reported that recidivism rates were substantially lower when the offender was arrested. According to police data, recidivism rates for arrested men after six months were 13% compared to 26% for offenders when police used the more traditional actions of mediation, "quieting the parties," or ensuring the assailant left the property (Sherman & Berk, 1984).

Similarly, in an ex-post facto design on 783 wife beating incidents, Berk and Newton (1985) found that when an officer made an arrest this appeared to reduce the number of new domestic violence incidents reported by that household.

General Deterrence

In addition to deterring existing offenders, arrest has been claimed to be an effective deterrent for potential abusers (Martin, 1978). This is based upon the observation that men, in general, have consistently ranked arrest as a potentially severe occurrence (Carmody & Williams, 1987; Dutton, 1988; Williams & Hawkins, 1989). In one study of anticipated indirect effects of an arrest for domestic violence, 63% of men stated they would suffer a loss of self-respect if arrested. Family stigma and social disapproval were also feared by most men. In contrast, time in jail or loss of a job were, accurately, not perceived as being likely after a domestic violence incident. Hence, while the possible ultimate costs of an arrest such as time in jail or loss of a job might be very severe, they were correctly perceived as being quite unlikely (Williams & Hawkins, 1989).

Deterrence theorists understand that this is predictable because formal sanctions such as conviction and sentencing for a domestic violence related crime may be far more serious than the simple act of an arrest. However, the chances of a conviction are so low that the deterrent effect is simply not credible. In contrast, the public perception, however inaccurate, of the capability and the inclination of police officers to make arrests may be the only effective available deterrent.

Other Rationales for Increasing the Use of Arrests

Impact Upon the Victim (Modifying Victim Behavior)

Increased use of arrest powers has also been advocated because of the potential impact upon the victim. An arrest for a specific domestic violence charge confirms the woman's status as a victim of a crime, not as merely another guilty participant of a battling family. The opposite effect may occur when the assailant previously was merely arrested for being drunk and disorderly. The label of being a victim may, in turn, increase her confidence in her rights and make her more likely to follow through with the prosecution process (Burris & Jaffe, 1983).

By placing the burden of prosecution on the state, less pressure is placed upon a victim who may already suffer from situational stress reactions, for example, Post Traumatic Stress Disorder. Also known as the Battered Woman Syndrome, this has been recognized as producing high levels of anxiety, panic attacks, and waves of depression. When the police take an initial action, the woman may be greatly relieved, both from having the immediate terror of the encounter removed as well as being freed from the responsibility of taking affirmative action against her oppressor.

Finally, such a policy may serve the needs of the victim and her friends and relatives to see retribution against her assailant. Although we may tend to discount the legitimacy of such motives (unless directly victimized by criminal behavior), this is one of the well-recognized purposes of the criminal justice system: to institutionalize retribution and obviate the need for vigilantism. Because ultimate conviction of an offender for a domestic violence crime remains to this date improbable, an arrest may serve as the only "punishment" the criminal justice system may realistically impose.

Impact Upon the Police (Modifying Police Behavior)

The increased use of arrest powers may have a critical effect on the attitudes of the police. As noted earlier, police have not considered the prevention of domestic violence to be a worthwhile police function. The act of making an arrest may, however, legitimize the function by providing the officer with a product for his efforts, an arrested offender (Stanko, 1989). Increased use of arrests might then make the response to domestic violence fit in with the law enforcement orientation of the police organization and subculture.

While possible, this theory would have to be tested by comparing attitudes of officers who have made arrests and in those organizations where making arrests are common, with attitudes of officers in other jurisdictions. Absent such evidence, we are not convinced arrests will "legitimize" police actions in the eyes of the police or reinforce the goal of committing officers to this task. Instead, it may be regarded in the police culture as a "garbage" arrest because it doesn't involve a "real" crime, does not require crime-solving skills, usually doesn't have any element of pursuit or apprehension of a dangerous offender, and ultimately, in most jurisdictions, will later result in the case being dismissed.

Other Indirect Effects (Modifying the Behavior of Society)

There may be an additional indirect impact upon society of a policy that favors arrest. Feminists and battered women's advocates have, as set forth in Chapter 1, observed that our culture "uses" domestic violence as another method of reinforcing the societal domination of men over women and children. The failure of police to arrest and courts to convict for wife battering is seen as tacitly condoning such conduct to put down the emerging aspirations of women and maintain the sexist order. A policy that favors using arrests in family settings might then serve to undermine one of the pillars of sexism in society, the implicit "right" of men to physically dominate women and children within his patriarchal family unit.

Society, however, need not fully subscribe to all of the tenets of feminism to realize that the increased use of arrests may have an affect on society. For example, it may well serve a boundary maintenance type of function. If police begin enforcing existing laws against domestic violence, gradually societal tolerance for such behavior may begin to dissipate as the behavior is labeled as a "crime." The direct analogy is to the increased enforcement of drunk driving laws in the past several years that has, by many accounts, led first to less toleration of drunk drivers by the public, and ultimately to fewer drunk drivers on the road.

This potential for societal change has not really been explored in the literature and may, at least at this time, be more of a hope rather than a reality. Writings of feminist academicians have not been widely publicized, perhaps because of sexism in the academic profession, or perhaps due to the stridency of the manner in which many deliver their message. Meanwhile, changes in arrest policies of particular police departments have not been well portrayed in the media. The general impression of the criminal justice response to the problem still reflects the classic pattern of indifference/hostility to intervention. Public knowledge of change within the system appears at this time to be restricted to police administrators, advocates of battered women, and researchers.

Is the Increased Emphasis on Arrests Misplaced?

Although the foregoing are cogent arguments for the use of arrest sanctions, the authors believe that arrests should have a restricted, albeit essential, role for police intervention in domestic assaults. We believe this for several reasons.

Does Deterrence Justify Arrest?

The key argument for increased use of arrest is its deterrent value. It is, however, unclear whether specific deterrence will occur.

Perhaps the primary problem with using arrest to deter future abuse is the premise of deterrence that the conduct sought to be deterred may be modified. Clearly, the strength of deterrence varies according to the nature of the offense. Illicit activities that are economically motivated or require careful planning would intuitively seem to be more amenable to deterrence. In contrast, it is probable that noneconomic crimes in general and the impulsive explosive use of violence typical in domestic assaults would least likely be deterred.

In stating this, the authors recognize that our operative assumptions about the etiology of family violence have led us to this conclusion. In contrast, many feminist authors believe that violent men can somehow control their outbursts. They find these men use violence as a weapon to establish dominance in settings where they are least likely to be punished, for example, the home, and can control the degree of violence that they use. We acknowledge this may be true for some, if not most, assailants. However, we continue to believe that it frequently is the stressful circumstances of the family that trigger the explosive violence of susceptible men or women.

In addition to only deterring those offenders that at some level are capable of limiting their conduct to "safe victims," the argument of the "humiliation" of an arrest as a deterrent advanced by Williams and Hawkins (1989) may only apply to certain groups. "Normal" citizens may indeed fear the humiliation of an arrest and its indirect effects. However, hard core "deviants" and those that have already been arrested for domestic violence or other charges are unlikely to be markedly deterred by yet another arrest (Ferraro, 1989). It can be argued that the latter group of hard core abusers accounts for the most numerous repetitive and severe acts of domestic violence (Pierce et al., 1988). Ford, using interview data, found that more than 95% of arrestees had previously battered the same victim, 94% in the previous six months (Ford, in press). Hard core offenders are therefore likely to be driven by factors not readily controllable.

The other category of offenders, situational deviates, might sporadically commit an act of domestic assault under great stress, but are not particularly likely to be recidivistic even if no intervention is made let alone the extreme use of an arrest. Hence, using arrest as a deterrent appears to have the most value in the group that needs it the least. Unfortunately, it would be conceptually and legally impossible to divide use of arrests between these groups. In fact, merely articulating a policy that favors arrest for a first time or "normal" offender but not for the hard core abuser graphically demonstrates its folly. Instead, such a policy can only be implemented as part of an overall framework heavily favoring arrests.

Placed in this framework, deterrence in the context of a domestic violence arrest depends upon the accuracy of a string of assumptions: (1) that deeply rooted noneconomically driven behavior can be consciously changed if an arrest occurs; (2) that the potential offender believes the police will be called; (3) the offender believes that police will respond and make an arrest; and (4) prospects for an arrest without any realistic probability of a conviction, or jail time, will act to inhibit conduct sufficient to prevent future abuse.

In this regard, Ford (1988) points out that domestic violence is usually an "impulsive act" drawn from a limited repertoire of responses to stress, attacks in self-esteem or frustration by those who have few inhibitions against using violence in angered states. Under such circumstances, it is difficult to argue that this will not reoccur if the same stress provoking factors arise in the future.

Will Deterrence Have a Lasting Impact?

The theory of deterrence in the context of long-term control of violent behavior is not consistent with current knowledge. Researchers who have addressed long-term treatment of these offenders have noted that deterrence depends upon the ability of coercive sanctions to prevent behavior. If, as we believe, many individual offenders undertake such action due to their own inadequacies, inability to express themselves, low self-esteem, and low inhibitions against violence (Star, 1982), it is difficult to discern what long-term rehabilitation will arise from the implied or expressed force used by an officer in the context of an arrest.

Although this has been shown in the recent replication studies of the Minneapolis Experiment discussed earlier, initially any exposure to the criminal justice system jolts an offender, causing short-term behavior modi-fication, however, it is unclear whether the effect is long term. In fact, recent research has suggested that in the case of domestic violence arrests, the impact of arrest on any offender may be transitory. Dutton (1987) found that being arrested appeared only to have an effect for six months, a relatively short period. Within 30 months, there was a 40% recidivism rate despite the arrest. Dutton concluded that any contact with the criminal justice system, unless reinforced by long-term counseling or other activities, might simply cause a relatively short-term behavioral change.

Perhaps the best long-term result that might be expected from an arrest is the modest achievement that fear of future punishment will facilitate com-pliance in attending a rehabilitation program. If, however, this is the limited and indirect deterrent value of an arrest, this might be accomplished not by arrest, but by the continued fear of punishment implied by more aggressive prosecution of a case no matter how it is brought to a court's attention.

Has Empirical Research Demonstrated Deterrence?

A critical examination of the empirical research that has supported the deterrent value of arrests simply does not appear to justify major policy changes. The Minneapolis study clearly was a well-designed, if limited, experiment with major policy implications. However, the design chosen and the limited sample of officers used made the internal and external validity of the study difficult to evaluate.

For example, the experimental precinct was plagued by high officer dropout rates with most arrests accounted for by a small proportion of police officers. Particular styles of intervention and differences in levels of training and commitment of these officers, as compared to the control groups, might therefore have easily accounted for the differences in subsequent offender behavior. Similarly, external validity of the original study is limited because the offender sample was heavily weighted toward a minority group population. Finally, the Minneapolis Police Department's policy at the time of the study to arrest and hold all such arrested offenders overnight in a police lockup, is highly unusual and may confound attempts to generalize the data (Binder & Meeker, 1988).

The strength of the association between rates of recidivism and the different methods employed is rather weak. One review of the original Sherman and Berk Minneapolis study reported that the experimental differences in the police response to domestic violence may have only accounted for approximately 1.8% of the total variance in recidivism rates (Binder & Meeker, 1988). Despite this being statistically significant, Binder et al. (1988), question the wisdom of basing policy on such a meager effect when it appears to explain a small amount of the behavioral variance.

Six replication studies of the Minneapolis Experiment have been undertaken in Omaha, Nebraska; Milwaukee, Wisconsin; Colorado Springs, Colorado; Charlotte, North Carolina; Atlanta, Georgia; and Dade County in Florida. While the results of most follow-up studies to the Minneapolis Experiment have yet to be released, the first city to release findings, Omaha, reported that there did not appear to be any significant difference in recidivism between arrested and non-arrested offenders (Omaha Police Department and NIJ, 1989).

Is Deterrence Without Rehabilitation a Worthwhile Goal?

We also question the underlying goal of a mechanistic application of deterrence theory. Even if arrest serves as a deterrent to spousal assault, without rehabilitation of the underlying tendency of an assailant toward outbursts of violence, the ultimate effect may be merely to displace the offender's violent tendencies. The offender may perceive that he can batter others, including children, aged relatives, or people in barroom brawls with less probability of police interference. Most pro arrest literature in contrast focuses solely on whether the arrest deters an offender from battering a specific victim. If, instead, the potential for displacement is considered, it is entirely possible that if no rehabilitation occurs and the perceived costs increase for abusing a particular partner due to a pro-arrest policy, the offender may simply terminate the relationship and enter into a relationship with a new prospective victim (Reis, 1986, in Elliott, 1989).

In a twist of this argument, it has been posited that if the victim finds that arrest does not deter subsequent assaults, she may be likely to leave. This may create a strong possibility that an unrehabilitated offender will simply abuse a different victim (Strube & Barbour, 1983, as quoted in Elliott, 1989). Under this assumption, deterrence without rehabilitation does not justify an increased role for arrests.

Does the Use of Arrest as a Deterrent Create Other Problems?

We believe that mandating arrests may have certain negative consequences. The cost effectiveness of the use of arrest should be considered. It cannot be disputed that arrests, especially if coupled with temporary incarceration, are costly to the law enforcement agency, to the offender, and often to the victim.

In addition to the rather obvious direct costs to the responding agency, an arrest of a family member, including an abusive spouse, is likely to be traumatic to other family members. Children may be traumatized by the arrest or the stigma associated with the event. This comment may, of course, be itself questioned by those who believe it may be *beneficial* for children to witness an arrest as it demonstrates that the conduct is not tolerated by society. We tend to believe, however, that there are few instances where a child who may closely identify with a parent would benefit by seeing him led out of the house in handcuffs any more than seeing him beating his other parent.

Although Sherman and Berk (1984) did not report such "secondary deviance," it is unclear whether this effect, even if real, would be found in a preliminary study using a six-month time frame. Assailants may begin identifying themselves as deviants, and a reverse spillover effect of this self-labeling may occur. While financial suffering of the family may not be frequent from an arrest itself, on occasion, the arrest may have an impact upon future employment, and more frequently, on child support or other payments made in the context of a "broken family."

Finally, the victim herself may feel the affects of an arrest. She may justifiably fear physical or economic retaliation or other acts designed to intimidate her from continuing to press charges. If already severely physically or emotionally traumatized by abuse, she may find the additional demands attendant to supporting an arrest beyond her capabilities. For such reasons, the prospects of an aggressive use of arrest powers may deter women from reporting future abuse.

It therefore is responsible to determine if other less intrusive measures would be of similar effectiveness with far fewer negative consequences. As noted earlier, virtually any police intervention, even if flawed, has some deterrent effect (Carmody & Williams, 1987; Pierce & Deutsch, in press; Feld & Straus, 1989; Ford, 1988).

The Victim Services Agency, in a 1988 training manual that strongly supported the increased use of arrests, noted that it was not clear whether the arrest per se was the critical factor. It was instead considered possible that merely giving the victim the apparent power to influence arrest decisions was the critical factor. It was considered possible that when the offender knew that the police followed victim preferences in making arrest, she was given power in her relationship, thereby lessening the possibility of future aggression. Conversely, when police ignored or were unaware of victim desires, a suspect might not modify his behavior even after an arrest occurred. Instead, he might believe that any police action was essentially arbitrary and unrelated to the victim's desires.

Finally, the authors have a philosophical concern over the use of an arrest as a punishment. Arrest used for its deterrent value appears to be a subversion of the legitimate but limited arrest powers constitutionally given to police.

The police have never constitutionally been given power to inflict "pain" and "humiliation" to effect social goals. Instead, there has been a recognition that no agency, especially the police, has this authority independent of established legal procedures to adjudicate guilt and prescribe standards of permissible official conduct. While it would be simplistic to ignore the daily informality inherent in dispensing "street level justice," and the travesty of cases such as Tracey Thurman's, making an arrest without an attendant commitment to prosecute those arrested appears to be a dangerous precedent. While it is recognized that the goal of deterrence of spousal assaults is sound and has been frustrated by past police inattention, we should be concerned that arrests have been often used in other contexts, such as the silencing of dissenters, or civil rights protestors.

HAVE THERE BEEN CHANGES IN STREET LEVEL ARREST PRACTICES?

Given the removal of structural barriers to arrest and the convergence of academic, political, and administrative pressures favoring arrest, one would expect a rapid increase in arrests in most jurisdictions. For a variety of reasons, such change has occurred sporadically without any consistent pattern. In Massachusetts, despite a broadening of police powers and heavy administrative pressure from state agencies and women's advocacy groups, few police encounters with domestic violence now result in arrest (Buzawa, 1990). Research that one of the authors conducted in Detroit, Michigan, in 1976 initially showed a noticeable decrease in incidents reported to the police during the 12 months after enactment of new legislation removing procedural barriers to arrest. This occurred despite the fact that the economy of Detroit was at the time declining, and shelter workers believed domestic violence was increasing (Buzawa, 1982). In fact, officer interviews in Detroit indicated that when they warned victims that an arrest would be made, if they were again called to the family, the "problem families" seemed to "quiet down," as measured by a lessening of their demands for police service. The danger is that police will often say, "If we come back, everyone goes to jail," perhaps on a disorderly conduct charge. This is an effective way to reduce repeat runs because victims won't call if they risk jail. When this is done, the police in effect invite batterers to continue battering with a reduced risk of interference. Thus, there is the possibility that a pro-arrest policy will lead to less protection of victims.

9

Mandatory Arrest Policies

WHERE ENACTED

In response to frustration over continued low arrest rates, despite statutory changes, the growing political pressure to "do something," and the dramatic impact of the Sherman and Berk Minneapolis study, many states and localities have considered or actually adopted legislation and ordinances that mandate arrests in certain cases of domestic violence. However, discretion as to when an officer should invoke the law is administratively common (and often ignored or minimized by individual officers). The enactment of a statute or ordinance to *mandate* agency action is highly unusual in criminal procedure. As such, it can readily be seen as a response to political pressure and a reaction to prior police inattention.

The following discussion focuses upon mandatory arrest policies, although Ferraro's interesting study of arrest practices in Phoenix concerned the results of a presumptive arrest policy. The distinction between the two types of policies is, however, important since a mandatory policy directs action and limits discretion, while a presumptive arrest policy simply serves to guide (albeit strongly) the officer's use of discretion in the direction of making an arrest. Further research will be needed to see what, if any, operational differences arise between the two types of policies.

Although this area is rapidly changing, as of early 1989, the following states have enacted such statutes. Virtually all such statutes apply to cases of felonies with some extending to certain misdemeanors or violation of protective orders (Table 9.1).

This statutory structure continues to rapidly change, as several states have adopted or considered such laws in the last legislative session, and statutory reference materials may be outdated. Also, as is common in this area, the statutes do not parallel each other with some requiring evidence of injury or other conditions.

In addition to the enactment of statutes mandating arrest practices, a number of police departments have administratively adopted a policy of mandatory or presumptive arrests in domestic violence cases. In 1984, only 15 out of 140 cities surveyed by the Crime Control Institute had policies

Table 9.1 These States Recently Enacted Mandatory Arrest Policies for Domestic Violence Offenders. The Level of Crime Charged Varies and Depends on Whether or Not the Crime Is a First Offense

Mandatory Arrest States	Application			
	Felony	Misdemeanor	For Violation of Restraining Order	For Primary Aggressor Only
Connecticut	*	* (if recent)	–	
Iowa	*	*	–	
Louisiana (only if victim in danger)	*	*	–	
Delaware	–	–	*	
Maine	*	–	*	
Nevada	*	*	*	
Minnesota	–	–	*	
New Jersey	*	*	–	
Oregon (first in country)	*	*	*	*
Washington	*	*	*	*
Wisconsin (only if victim in danger)	*	*	*	*
West Virginina	*	*	–	
North Carolina (for certain select categories)	–	–	*	

SOURCES: Victim Services Agency (1988) and MacManus and Hightower (1989).

encouraging arrests. After the original Sherman study received mass attention, this tripled by 1985 to 44 out of 140 cities surveyed (Binder & Meeker, 1988).

One study published in 1982 found that at that time, 47 "major" police departments had administratively adopted a mandatory or presumptive arrest policy. For example, Chicago officers are now being instructed to make arrests if any of the following factors are present: serious conflict, use of weapons, previous injury or property damage, previous court appearances, or involvement of children, retarded individuals, or intoxicated parties (Loving, 1980).

THE THEORETICAL BASIS FOR MANDATORY ARREST

The adoption of a mandatory arrest policy has been based on the belief that enactment of such policies will actually change street-level justice. The premise assumes that eliminating officer discretion is sufficient for such change to occur.

The proponents of such a policy do not necessarily believe that "abuse of discretion" is the only, or even the primary, problem with normal police practices. Instead, they believe that the basic problem is the inherent ambiguity of the police-citizen encounter in the context of a domestic violence call. The assumption is that the normal, and even proper use of discretion requires that an officer act on his or her values and experiences to make rapid interpretations of ambiguous facts, determine legal requirements, and analyze the consequences of possible actions. Only then is discretion applied to decide the proper course to follow. Here officers must decide whether to arrest, separate, or merely warn. In this context, it is theorized that the intervention of police in a normal "domestic call" will almost inevitably be colored and bounded by the "common knowledge" of the futility of police intervention. Hence, the use of discretion itself, not the abuse thereof, is said to make a mandatory policy preferable (Berk & Loseke, 1980-1981).

There is also a recognition by the framers of the legislation and administrative policies that most officers either do not have adequate knowledge of handling domestic violence cases, or actively disapprove of the concept of police intervention. Implementation of a rigid pro-arrest policy therefore tries to force change in behavior without necessarily changing officer attitudes. Attitudinal change, while apparently considered less important, would then occur at some later point, if at all, by training officers on the rationale of the policy and by "conversion" due to their immersion into the procedure.

It has also been noted that implementation of an arrest policy would have the collateral effect of increasing the likelihood that the arrested offenders would be convicted. Prosecutors and judges in general, and domestic violence cases in particular, have been said to disfavor continuing actions that were initiated by a victim instead of the police. One study reported that such cases are taken less seriously and far more frequently dropped than those cases brought in by the police (Burris & Jaffe, 1983). The accuracy of this observation has, however, been questioned by Ford (1987), and it is unclear whether it is an artifact of the sample studied or may instead be generalized.

The relevance of this point to mandatory arrests may be questioned. The arrest of a domestic violence offender in a mandatory arrest jurisdiction might be treated as being similar to those brought in by private complaints since, for this one specific crime, a prosecutor would not have to face a potentially irate police officer asking why "his" case was dropped without a charge.

Positive effects of a mandatory arrest policy have also been predicted by proponents for both victims and offenders. One article theorized that without such a policy, women have become disillusioned with the police, feeling they cannot be protected and as a result, do not even call them (Burris & Jaffe, 1983). Similarly, if the premise is accepted that arrest does deter further violence, then adoption of a mandatory arrest policy should provide even a higher level of deterrence (Burris & Jaffe, 1983).

HAS A MANDATORY ARREST POLICY AFFECTED POLICE BEHAVIOR?

Little research has demonstrated that a mandatory arrest policy will have its intended effect. One study in Oregon has, however, tentatively reported evidence that there were 10% fewer domestic violence assaults, and the percentage of homicides among people of the known relationships dropped from 37% to 27% following the implementation of a 1977 mandatory arrest law, despite regional economic strains that would normally be predictive of higher rates of domestic violence (Jolin, 1983; also quoted in the U.S. Attorney General's Task Force on Family Violence, *Final Report*, 1984). However, the small sample size of Jolin's study and the fact that homicides decreased in the year before the new law took effect, make its findings difficult to generalize from. While this data is suggestive, it is by no means conclusive. Instead, it deals with a change from the historical statutory and policy structure that disfavored police involvement in mandatory arrests.

It would be informative to examine the impact of a modernized statutory framework coupled with a progressive administration. The impact of modern pre-service and in-service training programs as well as the removal of administrative bias against domestic violence calls could then be assessed. Without such an effort, an erroneous conclusion about the need for mandatory policies may be found.

Further studies should also be undertaken both in the context of alternate policies and also to review recidivism and police arrest rates over an extended time. This could better determine if the effects of a mandatory arrest policy are merely transitory until offenders have adapted to a new police response, and if the rank and file police have developed mechanisms to circumvent statutory limitations on their discretion.

One obvious factor is that to achieve any effect on rates of abuse, one necessary intermediate outcome is that change must occur in police practices after enactment of a mandatory arrest policy. Results in this regard are inconclusive. The Victim Services Agency in 1988 stated that there could be no doubt that such laws where enacted led to a huge increase in cases being handled by the criminal justice system. In support, researchers studying police practices in London, Ontario, reported that there was a 2,500% increase in the rate of arrests following a new mandatory arrest policy (Jaffe et al., 1986). While this sounded dramatic, the policy had also expanded the officer's ability to make warrantless arrests so that some increase was to be expected. In addition, the number arrested after the new policy constituted only 9% of total domestic violence calls. The disparity between the policy and the reality was apparently due to an increasing tendency of officers to fail to find "reasonable and probable grounds" for an arrest.

Similarly, after the State of Washington enacted a mandatory arrest law, the arrest rate increased fourfold, the number of cases doubled, and the number of cases set for trial and actually prosecuted tripled (Victim Services Agency, 1988, citing figures reported by The Family Violence Project of the Seattle City Attorney's Office). This does show that an effect on officer behavior occurred; however, it has not been subject to rigorous analysis of the type and quality of arrests made. The only other research in that state shows that there was an unprecedented increase in "dual arrests," where both spouses were arrested. One estimate was that one-third of all arrests made were dual arrests—hardly the result hoped for by advocates of change (Epstein reported in Victim Services Agency, 1988).

Even the Minneapolis Police Department, an enthusiastic supporter of the use of arrests, acknowledged that in 1986, despite a mandatory arrest policy, out of 24,948 domestic assault calls, only 3,645 arrests were reported, or less than 20% (Balos & Trotzky, 1988). Instead, according to police reports, in 60% of these incidents, the officer disposed of the case through "talk" or "mediation" with suspects arrested only about 22% of the time. In addition, according to a reported citizen survey, in 12% of the cases, the police did not even respond to the call. In still other cases, an officer responded but failed to file the report required by policy (Balos & Trotzky, 1988). Studies in other jurisdictions have confirmed that officers rarely make misdemeanor arrests despite a new statute mandating such an outcome.

This does not mean, however, that no change has occurred. The key is that there is now even less consistency and predictability of officer actions. Instead, the primary characteristic of the police response to domestic violence today is its inherent unpredictability. This is in contrast to the past when inaction or apathy was the norm (see also Berk & Loseke, 1980-1981; Stanko, 1989; Worden & Pollitz, 1984).

There are several reasons for such varied results. The most commonly cited is the failure of legislators to devise any effective plan to implement new pro-arrest policies. The statutes appear to be prepared primarily at the request of national and feminist groups. Sporadic support is received from local and state organizations, shelter and advocacy groups, senior "progressive" police officials, and the efforts of federally funded agencies, foundations, and researchers.

Although difficult to empirically measure, it does not appear that the desires, frustrations, or organizational reality confronting line managers and the rank and file police were considered in formulating such statutes. This is critical because it has been generally acknowledged that line officers in large departments are already distrustful of orders based on outside political pressure, and what appears to be the whim of departmental leadership.

Although nominally constrained by rigid rules, officers have become adept at circumventing rules, laws, and polices that are not in conformance with their underlying beliefs. During the course of responding to accelerated requests for change, this extends to ignoring or subverting recognized rules of criminal procedure, or explicit organizational goals and directives (Manning, 1977; Stanko, 1989). The result is that the officers may merely become more careful with their paperwork to simply ensure the report "covers" them while they continue with their desired response.

In this case, the underlying assumption of most rank and file officers is that making arrests in domestic violence cases is, at best, futile, and, at worst, counterproductive. Absent an organizationally positive environment of total supervision, officers appear to continue to rely on cues derived from victims and offenders to decide whether a law has been broken and, if so, whether an arrest should be made (Ferraro, 1989b). If they so choose, they can easily report that they failed to detect the elements of probable cause to justify an arrest.

Apart from general strictures "mandating" training, little concern or subsequent funding has been placed upon law implementation. For example, 10 states—California, Massachusetts, Maine, Missouri, Nebraska, Ohio, Pennsylvania, Washington, Wisconsin, and Wyoming—mandate police training on domestic violence. No state, however, provided consistent funding for such training. As a result, training on the necessity for arrest has tended to be sporadic and inconsistent across departments. If funding was initially provided through state funding, it was typically for an initial period allowing for curriculum development. No continued operational funds were provided, and police departments often were forced to abandon such programs. Due to constant officer turnover, this quickly diluted the value of the initial training. In Detroit, for example, there was almost a 50% turnover of patrol officers in a three-year period, and budgetary pressures forebade giving any relevant domestic violence training after the first classes.

Another factor has been the lack of control over training content. Research on the impact of training after legislative changes in Minnesota were not encouraging. An observer noted that the content contributed to the existing negative attitudes toward female victims and was in conflict with the intent of the statutes (Pastoor, 1984).

Other studies have not confirmed that long-term changes in street-level police practices will occur after enactment of a mandatory arrest statute. Rank and file police have well-developed strategies to resist "unwarranted" interference. They may continue to believe that domestic violence is a "normal" part of some deviant groups and that intervention is futile. Ferraro (1989a) examined the presumptive arrest policy in Phoenix, Arizona, and confirmed that virtually all male officers disliked the policy. Most female officers were, at best, neutral or even antagonistic (Ferraro, 1989a).

It appears that an unpopular policy can readily be circumvented. An officer could fail to "find" the requisite cause to make an arrest. Some officers required visible injuries to report "probable cause." This is definitely not necessary for establishing probable cause for commission of a misdemeanor. Hence, a standard more appropriate for a felony has been adopted to execute a misdemeanor arrest. The redefinition of observed conduct may be unintentional if the officer truly believes his actions are in his and the department's interests and even the best interests of the victim.

Another method of avoidance is simply not to pursue an arrest when an offender has left the scene. In two cities, Phoenix and Omaha, approximately one-half of all offenders left when the police were called (Omaha Police Department Press Release, 9/9/89; Ferraro, 1989a). In Phoenix, of the 40% of the cases where offenders had left, there were no reports completed, and in most of the other cases the information was so sketchy that follow-up was impossible (Ferraro, 1989a). Undoubtedly, other methods to avoid such a policy will be followed in other circumstances.

In addition to passive resistance of the rank and file, implementation strategies have a real impact upon actual performance. In Phoenix, it took the police chief's direct involvement before any change occurred. For the first 3 weeks of the presumptive arrest policy, the arrest rate of 18% was less than the prearrest rate of 33%. That rate went up to 67% only after the chief intervened and personally instructed officers that he was in fact committed to the policy. Officer behavior then changed with a subsequent increase in arrests.

However, the judiciary soon objected to the wave of "ridiculous arrests." Subsequently, a departmental clarification was promulgated that clarified the necessity for probable cause. Although this might not have been the officially desired result, the officers apparently took the clarification to mean "business as usual." Accordingly, the arrest rate quickly dropped back to 42%—close to the pre-policy arrest rate (Ferraro, 1989a). Obviously, this result could be an artifact of difficulties in implementation. However, we believe this to be unlikely; a more probable result was that the officers seized upon any weakness or hint of a lack of resolve to erode the disfavored policy. At a minimum, any analysis of a mandatory or presumptive arrest policy must also carefully review the possible impact of the implementation strategies followed, and must conduct an analysis for a sufficient period to determine short- and long-term behavioral impact.

DOES A MANDATORY ARREST POLICY IMPOSE UNACCEPTABLE COSTS?

The adoption of a mandatory arrest policy cannot be decided without considering potential costs that may arise if organizational change actually occurs and the number of arrests increases. We do not believe that a mandatory arrest policy is desirable. There are five major reasons for this position.

First, it is clear to us that such a policy would markedly increase costs to public agencies arguably without demonstrable benefits. We find no basis for believing that aggregate numbers of convictions will increase. If a victim does not want to prosecute, she may merely refuse to testify. If forced to testify, she may recount events that occurred in a manner that fails to justify a conviction (Ferraro, 1989b). Meanwhile, arrest costs are high. Several senior officers have estimated to the authors that three to four man-hours are needed for each arrest. This time commitment would, of course, escalate by orders of magnitude if court proceedings are undertaken but later dropped.

In stating this, we realize that even a cursory study of the Thurman case and similar cases throughout the country may convince even the most skeptical that past police practices have been both inadequate and exceptionally callous toward domestic violence victims in many jurisdictions. However, it still is appropriate that advocates of any change requiring substantially more time from an agency explain how this will be achieved. It is a truism that most police departments are overworked and understaffed. We believe that advocates of mandatory arrest should go beyond discussing past police failings, and instead be forced to identify the current tasks of the police department that should be abandoned or scaled back to accommodate the extra time commitments that would arise if a mandatory arrest policy actually is practiced (as opposed to merely being "on the books.") Such an analysis may lead to a realization that greater emphasis should be placed upon the *quality* of the intervention, perhaps using arrests in all cases where probable cause exists and the victim desires an arrest, not a mechanistic forced arrest policy that the victim doesn't desire and the police officer believes (even if incorrect) is counterproductive.

Second, unintended adverse consequences of a mandatory arrest policy may arise. The current police frustration at their inability to help abused women may intensify at the real additional costs of a mandatory arrest policy.

Call screening or other techniques to avoid an arrest would dramatically increase, leaving some victims without any recourse to the police. The net result may therefore be to shift help from some victims who receive no police assistance to another group who obtain the degree and type of help that a paternalistic system believes is appropriate, whether desired or not.

Third, we strongly believe that victim preferences should be considered in formulating any policy. Police have frequently been criticized for indifference to victim wishes. A mandatory arrest policy merely appears to make victims and assailants pawns to larger policy goals formulated by administrators and well-meaning "victim advocates," whose goals may not be shared. Despite her emotional involvement and trauma, the victim is usually in a better position than patrol officers to determine the likely impact of an offender's arrest.

It appears presumptuous that "women's rights" advocates can determine what is best for the entire category of battered women. Whether imagined or real, concerns of economic harm or physical retaliation may cause many, but not all, abused women to disfavor an arrest. Clearly, she wants the beatings to end yet she may justifiably desire to control the outcome of the legal intervention. The denial of her own essential autonomy has even been viewed as "a new form of male chauvinistic domination" (Stanko, 1989).

In stating the foregoing, we understand that police must be trained to privately ask the victim for her preference and ensure she is unheard by the assailant. They must also have sufficient skill to convince her they will not tell the assailant of her preference. We believe that a competent training program can, however, address these concerns.

The elimination of victim control may also have unexpected side effects. Once a woman realizes that she loses control over the arrest outcome, she may herself be deterred from calling the police (Buzawa, 1982). After the initiation of a more aggressive arrest policy, an examination of aggregate arrest data for domestic assaults in Detroit indicated that fewer calls for assistance were received than before the policy. Consequently, there were fewer arrests, although the proportion of calls to arrests did increase. Available evidence did not suggest that the actual rate of domestic violence was decreasing. Instead, interviewed officers and command officials stated their belief that the same problem families existed but that the victim often no longer called the police. This was partially attributed to their fear of losing power to determine the outcome of the police intervention. As occurred in a jurisdiction where the officer had the discretion to be influenced by victim preference, victim deterrence is likely to intensify in a mandatory arrest jurisdiction (Buzawa, 1982). We do not believe that victim deterrence, although reducing the pressure on police resources, would be viewed favorably by advocates of mandatory arrest.

Fourth, a mandatory arrest policy places far more power in the hands of the police departments, who have historically been unsympathetic to the needs and goals of abused women. One could easily surmise that this might result in the adoption of mechanistic approaches to create unanticipated outcomes that might even be injurious to the abused party. For example, when called to the scene of a domestic disturbance, police often confront low-intensity conflicts such as a fist fight or other evidence of "battling spouses." If a mandatory arrest policy is mechanistically invoked, police may (and have) effectively deterred victims by not too subtly hinting that both parties will be arrested if the situation does not immediately calm down or if called again to the location. This authority would be within their rights since women have often initiated violence and Equal Protection demands that the male not be arbitrarily discriminated against. This, however, is not likely to be a result favored by most advocates of mandatory arrest.

While this might appear to be an artificial or exaggerated objection, there is substantial evidence that this occurs. A study on the mandatory arrest law in the State of Washington found that fully one-third of all arrests were dual arrests. In 50% of cases where any arrest was made, the woman was charged (Epstein, 1987). Other studies reported by the Victim Services Agency showed a dual arrest rate of 11% in Oregon and 18.8% in Connecticut. Although at first startling, these results are perhaps to be expected. If police are not allowed discretion in the arrest decision, they are unlikely to do so for a much narrower jurisdiction of self-defense. Instead, they simply arrest both parties and "let the judge sort it out." While "primary aggressor" modifications to the statutes might alleviate the problem of dual arrests, they would in turn also reintroduce the element of police discretion that they attempted to eliminate.

In addition to the dilemma of "battling spouses," police have undoubtedly encountered false cross complaints of violence that could not be disproven. In a mandatory arrest jurisdiction, these are likely to result in the arrest of the victim as well as of the offender. An officer that arrested only one party despite being confronted with two claims of abuse may be subject to liability.

Finally, the police might make spurious arrests of victims on trivial "disorderly person" charges if exasperated with repeat calls from an address or confronted with a verbally abusive woman. This may occur even though it would obviously constitute a serious misuse of powers. In any event, the effect of an arrest upon a victim of domestic violence is obvious. It is difficult to imagine a greater victim deterrent to calling the police than being arrested as a result of such a call.

Finally, as previously discussed, a mandatory arrest policy may perversely lessen the inclination of judges to seriously treat domestic violence calls. In her Phoenix study, Ferraro (1989a) reported that police were told to make an arrest if either party destroyed the couple's community property. A frustrated woman tore her dress in front of officers and was promptly arrested for "destruction of community property." Naturally, judges complained of these "ridiculous arrests." The resulting policy clarification created great uncertainty both for the judiciary and the department and tended to trivialize cases clearly warranting arrest (Ferraro, 1989a).

10

Training Programs

The final major innovation in the police response to domestic violence has been the rapid growth of extensive training programs. As described earlier, most jurisdictions previously gave little effective domestic violence training to their officers. In contrast, many states now statutorily mandate or "encourage" the development and implementation of police domestic violence training programs for all recruits and often for administrators (Hendricks, 1988). It is anticipated that exposure to skilled training will create or enhance attitudes that will prepare the police for a more activist role.

WHY DEVOTE RESOURCES TO TRAINING?

Effective domestic violence training requires a substantial training investment. Attempts to change deeply ingrained behavior reinforced by strong organizational pressure may be more difficult than the transmission of rules, regulations, and policies. Proponents of such programs justify the cost as follows. First, if police, as in most jurisdictions, are to retain the discretion to decide appropriate actions and the determination of an arrest, they need a working knowledge of the causes of domestic violence, intervention strategies, legal requirements for their actions, and the policies adopted by their own particular departments. Without such training, police will continue to be plagued with the nonuniform and substandard response characteristic of the past.

Second, even if statutory goals of more police intervention in domestic violence cases is not shared by a particular department's leadership, training in conformity with enacted domestic violence legislation reduces the possibility of lawsuits and limits departmental liability for particularly negligent conduct by individual officers.

Third, if the department is in a jurisdiction that has adopted new procedural or substantive grounds for making arrests, training is essential to communicate the existence and rationale of such requirements. Both elements are essential given the capability of rank and file officers to subvert legislative intent if so motivated.

WHAT IS THE STATE OF TRAINING EFFORTS AT THIS TIME?

Although a full review of existing training programs has not been completed to date, several observations may be made. Domestic violence training is not presently standardized. Many different formats are currently followed with markedly different content, duration, and instructors' skill mix. For example, the authors have found that instructor qualifications for these programs still vary considerably. Some use dedicated teams of police academy instructors, outside care providers, and college/university lecturers. Others still rely on relatively untrained senior officers forced to teach because of limited duty assignments, budget restrictions, or other organizational needs.

In addition to lack of uniformity in instructors, the program content varies considerably. Some departments are using curriculum training materials developed by the Victim Services Agency in 1988 and disseminated through nationwide seminars. Others, as in Rochester, New York, and Detroit, Michigan, are using their own resources to develop training materials and often utilize sophisticated media aids. Some departments still continue to use short presentations of "war stories" by senior officers.

The training program may not even reflect the policy goals of departmental administrators. Pastoor (1984, p. 599) observed training in Minnesota following the new domestic violence statute mandating arrest for violation of protective orders, and provisions allowing police to arrest with probable cause in misdemeanor cases. Despite state requirements that officers be trained to understand when arrests may and must be made, Pastoor observed their training and found it "minimizes and discredits arrest as an appropriate response to battered women." Alternatives to arrest such as mediation were still stressed, and arrest was recommended only as a last resort. Hence, the training program was in direct contradiction to the apparent goals of the legislation and could hardly be expected to reinforce its intent (Pastoor, 1984).

WHAT EFFECT DOES TRAINING HAVE ON THE POLICE?

Although it has been hypothesized that differences in course content and instruction lead to behavior differences in officers, little available research has been conducted across departments. Buzawa (1988) did report results of an examination of the effect of training in various departments in New Hampshire, Massachusetts, and Detroit. Differences in training appeared to determine whether a particular program was effective in promoting attitudinal changes. In Detroit, officers attended a comprehensive in-service training program devoted to family violence. The response of officers attending that program initially appeared to be consistent with the departmental goals. However, in those New Hampshire departments where the training was not comprehensive, it appeared to have little impact upon officer response. While there were significant variations among the different departments, there were surprisingly similar responses within departments. Thus, officers may be more responsive to administrative policies and operational cases than training. However, this study would need to be replicated over a longer time period and in numerous different jurisdictions to make any conclusions more definitive (Buzawa, 1988).

It is also still largely uncertain what long-term impact domestic violence training has upon officer attitudes and behavior. Some results are encouraging. It has been reported that there are significant attitudinal changes of police recruits toward the proper police response to violence on the basis of being exposed to a relatively intensive training class on the subject (Buchanan & Perry, 1985). These researchers observed that after attendance at a five-day domestic violence training program, District of Columbia recruits expressed marked changes in their perceptions toward domestic violence disputes. They subsequently believed that responding to domestic violence calls was legitimate police business, police officer intervention could be effective, and people in crisis wanted and needed their assistance. The researchers' conclusion was that domestic violence training should indeed be stressed. However, the study was limited since it was conducted from a police recruit sample, not the more jaundiced population of experienced officers.

Elliott (1989) summarized existing research and noted that training police in mediation techniques increased police use of referrals to outside agencies and an increased "dispatch" rate. He also reported that training appeared to reduce the incidence of unreported assaults upon police, a goal that many police administrators might believe sufficient to justify training. However, Elliott did not find that overall arrest rates changed or that training in use of mediation techniques reduced the risk of subsequent violence between the parties.

Similarly, one study in Detroit, Michigan, reported that training has apparently affected officer attitudes and behavior. Buzawa (1981) found that exposure to Detroit's in-service police training program on domestic violence was the only variable that significantly predicted officer/respondent's expressed attitude toward domestic violence intervention. Although the program was in many respects advanced and appeared to be quite effective, budgetary pressures, as in many cities, ultimately forced its cancellation.

Such termination may prove the ultimate irony of training programs. Although considerable resources may be devoted to developing and administering a program, in-service police training is not considered essential to police administrators. Under such circumstances, these programs risk being curtailed or even abandoned during the next almost inevitable budget crisis.

11

Changes in Prosecutorial and Judicial Response

The process of change in the judicial response to family violence has not been as comprehensive or as advanced as in the case of the police. For the reasons discussed previously, virtually every state has passed some form of comprehensive statute dealing with the criminal justice response to domestic violence. These statutes typically contain provisions that allow judges to issue protective orders in appropriate domestic violence cases, and further expand the substantive criminal law provisions to give prosecutors and the judiciary more flexibility to adequately sanction inappropriate conduct. These changes, which will be discussed, have clearly removed significant impediments to effective judicial action.

There are two major differences between implementation of such statutes by the police and the prosecutor/judiciary. The police, however grudgingly, are expected to follow the law as it is written. The prosecutors, while clearly sworn to uphold laws, have expressly been given the powers to use their discretion in enforcement. In cases where the particular prosecutor does not happen to share the value judgments embodied in a statute, it is relatively simple for him or her to use discretion and merely not charge an offender or fail to take a victim's requested action. Similarly, judges have the express responsibility to adjudicate the conduct of a particular offender as well as interpret and rule on the constitutionality of laws. Many judges are unsympathetic with the values of proponents of domestic violence legislation and disturbed by the impingement of an offender's rights. They have the ability to refuse to enforce the statute, and the rights of a victim to contest the actions of a criminal court judge are virtually nonexistent.

Virtually all researchers and administrators have agreed that the police need to exercise a more activist position. Disagreement is largely confined to the issue of the proper role of arrest and the measures needed to effect the desired policy. Many prosecutors and judges believe they have already

110

devoted sufficient resources to this problem given overwhelming time demands from other types of crimes. Consequently, the consensus needed to force systemic change has not yet transpired. This has imparted a degree of uncertainty in the judicial response exceeding that of the police.

Although many articles have been published by victim rights advocates, feminist attorneys, and law review editors that strongly urge further change, issues of operational performance of the prosecutor and the judiciary have not captured the attention of the public or state legislatures. As a result, prosecutorial and judicial mismanagement of domestic violence cases has never gained saliency. The only possible exception has been the sporadic outcry to an occasional outrageous unguarded public comment made by an isolated trial court judge. There is a strong possibility that such attitudes are not atypical but are endemic and systematized. The treatment of women in general, and domestic violence victims in particular, by many prosecutors and the judiciary has never been understood by the public. Similarly, since most commentaries on the judicial response have been published in law journals or "advocacy" publications and are based on nonquantitative measures, research results have not yet been mobilized to effect change. Therefore, operational change that has occurred is more a product of the orientation and training of individual administrators, rather than a concerted enforced mandate or a nationwide trend.

Although innovative programs are initially financed by a federal or state grant, they ultimately become the financial responsibility of the locality. Since such innovations are not demanded by the public or by law, they often become victim to the widespread budget exigencies present in the public sector. We will discuss several major changes now being evaluated and adopted, including attempts to reduce case dismissal rates by improving the operation of the prosecutor's officer, and the effort to systematically divert appropriate cases out of the criminal justice system through mediation and court-mandated counseling. However, for the reasons outlined, such efforts are not systematically adopted or in practice at the present time.

PROTECTIVE ORDERS

The Increased Reliance on Prior Restraint

One of the significant recent innovations in judicial responses to domestic violence has been the adoption of statutes allowing judges to grant injunctive orders to immediately stop abuse. These may be permanent or preliminary in nature, or orders of shorter duration called temporary restraining orders or

TROs, for relief prior to a hearing necessary for a permanent injunction. These statutes have been patterned after the 1976 *Protection From Abuse Act Pa. Stat. Ann.* 35 sec. 10181-10890. They allow a court to hold hearings and issue a permanent protective order forbidding specific future conduct by the restrained person or a preliminary order without any formal court decision.

Courts have had the power to issue injunctive decrees for many decades. However, until specific domestic violence statutes were passed, their use was very infrequent in the context of prevention of domestic assault. In addition, many of the new statutes criminalized enforcement of the order.

Protective orders differ from a criminal prosecution in three areas: (1) protective orders are heard in civil courts, not criminal courts; (2) civil rules of procedure apply with the evidentiary standard being a "preponderance" of the evidence rather than beyond a reasonable doubt (Finn, 1989); and (3) the hearing is explicitly designed to separate the parties and prevent future unlawful conduct rather than punish past criminal behavior (Finn, 1989). Although protective orders are usually issued by civil courts, they are of direct relevance to the criminal justice system as their violation may be punishable by contempt of court and enforcement in many jurisdictions may be through an arrest, that is, the enforcement is criminalized. In 1989, violation of protective orders constituted an independent ground for justifying a warrantless arrest in 19 states. In other states, it remains punishable by contempt of court. Contempt of court, the traditional mechanism for enforcement, is slow and cumbersome but may allow invocation of severe punishment including jail.

Protective orders originate out of the civil powers of a general purpose court to adjudicate disputes, and/or a specialized family court's authority to resolve marital and familial matters. Although not directly related to their primary powers, criminal courts in at least one jurisdiction have been given the power to issue permanent and preliminary injunctions and temporary restraining orders. Violation of these orders may, in turn, subject an offender to a warrantless arrest. In 1977, New York state gave both criminal courts and county courts concurrent jurisdiction over domestic violence with equal powers to issue temporary restraining orders and permanent injunctions. This has the potential for dramatically enhancing the criminal court's ability to divert appropriate cases from the criminal justice system. It may also serve as a model for judges who might seek to impose a "no contact" order as a condition of probation. No analysis has been made of the use of this power by criminal courts of their new prejudgment injunctive powers or how other jurisdictions have considered or adopted this change. With the dramatic caseload increase of the state courts of New York, we can surmise that use of these new powers might actually be constrained unless administration is very routinized.

The power to issue this type of injunctive order is considered ancillary to the court's substantive powers. Because the issuance of such orders is not the court's primary purpose, judges have historically used them sparingly. They are primarily initiated at the request of a prosecutor or in civil courts by an attorney representing the claimant to limit uncontrollable threats by the person being restrained.

Courts typically attempt representation of both parties at a hearing prior to issuance of any permanent or even preliminary injunctions. If the matter is urgent, such as the threat of immediate violence, 37 states have authorized short-term *ex-parte* orders. They are usually in effect for no more than 10 days if the order is issued without the alleged offender being present and only the complainant attends.

Several types of domestic violence related protective orders have become common in domestic violence cases. General civil protection orders or TROs have been adopted for these cases by 48 states and the District of Columbia (all states except Arkansas and New Mexico). In addition, most states have enacted protection orders ancillary to a divorce or other marital proceeding. Although specific statutes vary, most require some prior evidence of the likelihood of improper conduct prior to issuance of an order, for example, either actual or serious threats of physical abuse to the plaintiff-divorcee or children.

The broad scope of marital orders parallels that of the generalized protective order statutes. Since these may be coupled with interim custody and support orders, the range of remedies may be even wider.

Advantages of Protective Orders

The scope of civil protective orders gives such instruments the potential for assuming a central role in the response to domestic violence. This is true for six reasons.

First, the courts have far wider discretion to fashion injunctive relief, unlike the relatively strict sentencing restraints in criminal cases. Thirty-eight states have expressly given judges the authority to grant "any constitutionally warranted relief that is available" (Finn, 1989). For example, courts often issue the following protective orders in domestic violence cases:

- Orders to refrain from other physical or psychological abuse or even to restrict any contact with an alleged victim;
- Orders to vacate a domicile within a certain period or to allow the alleged victim the exclusive use of certain personal property, such as a car, even though title to the property is in the name of the restrained party;
- Orders to enter counseling;

- Orders to pay support, restitution, or attorney fees;
- Orders granting temporary custody of minors to the victim—available in 40 states and the District of Columbia by 1989; and
- Orders limiting visitation rights to minor children.

This list should not, however, be viewed as exhaustive. A court's power to restrain improper conduct is not limited to any particular remedy, but is intended to be applied to the specific situation. The order may be fashioned to prevent circumstances that have previously led to violence.

Second, protective orders give the judicial system an opportunity to prospectively intervene to prevent likely abuse. This avoids the necessity of requiring recalcitrant bureaucracies and often reluctant victims to try to prove past criminal conduct beyond a reasonable doubt. This is particularly useful for cases where threats, intimidation, or prior misdemeanor activity suggest that the potential for serious future abuse is quite high.

Third, in those states where enforcement of the order has been criminalized, the existence of the order itself provides a potent mechanism for police to stop abuse, that is the right to arrest and subsequently convict for violation of its terms. The officer should easily recognize that the elements of a *prima-facie* case of violation of a "no contact" TRO are much easier to prove than violation of an assault statute based solely upon conduct occurring before the officer arrived on the scene.

The use of protective orders should also make it more likely that police will act decisively. It gives police departments a method for recognizing when an offender is a recidivist, and provides evidence that the victim is willing to initiate legal action to stop the conduct, thereby justifying an increased response.

More cynically, when the police respond to a domestic violence incident where a protective order is in existence, they may be more inclined to take action. Otherwise, the terms of an order might later be presented by the victim's counsel to establish a duty of care that the officer owed the victim. Breach of this duty would in turn potentially make the officer or his police department civilly liable if the order is not enforced.

Fourth, obtaining a protective order from a court has the effect of increasing the leverage and relative power of the victim. Specifically, she may obtain relatively unfettered control over the home or other essential assets. In states that have given police enforcement powers, the knowledge that an order can be enforced by the local police department may make her more secure and the offender less likely to resume any abuse.

The victim, if determined or assisted by a knowledgeable advocate, has the potential for far more control of the proceedings than in a prosecution. After obtaining a protective order, she can overcome indifference or even the hostility of police, prosecution, and court personnel, if not judges. She can also retain more control by using or withholding the injunction or by not alerting police to a violation. Although it might appear to be quixotic to obtain and then not actually use an injunction, this may be the only method in a state that has adopted a mandatory arrest policy for the victim to prevent the system from inexorably gaining total control over her affairs.

Fifth, civil protective orders do not present some of the costs to the victim incurred by a criminal prosecution. Specifically, the mere issuance of a protective order does not jeopardize the job of an offender as might a conviction and possible jail sentence for a crime. Hearings are less likely to require a time commitment from the victim. Fear of offender retaliation should lessen significantly since harm from violating a protective order is prospective in nature. Thus the offender may be constantly reminded by the victim what might happen if he violates the order rather than bitterly remember a punishment that has already been inflicted.

Sixth, divorce-related injunctive orders have an additional unique role. They are available when women are represented by counsel who is at least familiar with obtaining injunctive orders. Family court or domestic relations judges and court personnel are also frequently knowledgeable about the scope of, and protection against, domestic violence. In addition, even in no-fault divorce states, the family judge makes property allocations in the absence of the parties' agreement and decides the contested custody disputes. Under such circumstances, obtaining a protective order may deter future contact (and modify the offender's previously uncontrollable behavior).

LIMITATIONS OF PROTECTIVE ORDERS

Despite statutory provisions to use protective orders in domestic violence cases, several factors limit their relevance. First, the actual issuance of an order is, with few exceptions, at the judge's discretion. Although the legislative intent may be to grant such orders freely when needed, courts have always considered pre-judgment injunctive relief as a significant restriction on personal liberty, and as ancillary to their primary judicial duties. (Quinn, 1985; Waits, 1985). They are not issued as a matter of course, and judges usually require the prior commission of serious acts of domestic violence prior to issuing an order. This reluctance is naturally increased when an ex-parte order of the type common in a TRO is considered. Because such an order significantly restricts a defendant's liberty and property rights, he is constitutionally protected in his right to due process from its arbitrary issuance.

The primary legal critique of ex-parte orders is that they have deprived the defendant of his constitutional rights. For example, the Administrative Judge of the New York City Family Court in 1985 circulated a memorandum to all family court judges in New York City stating that

> the propriety of issuing such an order without . . . notice to petitioners raises I believe due process questions because this practice denies petitioners timely notice of respondent's allegations and an opportunity to prepare an adequate defence. . . . Although this issue is certainly within the discretion of each judge, I urge that you discuss the above . . . (to) be aware of the consequences of their issuing . . . orders of protection (Golden, 1987).

Constitutional arguments are based upon a series of United States Supreme Court cases wherein ex-parte prejudgment orders were questioned for due process reasons. Without exploring these in depth, it appears the United States Supreme Court has mandated that all such ex-parte actions must balance the private rights being abridged with the governmental reasons for its action, the intrinsic fairness of the existing proceedings, and the probable value of providing additional safeguards *Mathews vs. Eldridge* 424 US 319, 1976, citing *Fuentes vs. Shevin* 407 US 67, 1972; and *Mitchell vs. W.T. Grant Co.* 416 IS 600, 1974).

Although the United States Supreme Court has not ruled on the constitutionality of domestic violence protective orders, a series of state court rulings suggest that they will be upheld. For example, *Boyle vs. Boyle* 12 Penn D & C 3rd 767 (1979) upheld an ex-parte order forbidding the husband from entering the couple's jointly owned home. Similarly in *State ex rel. Williams vs. Marsh* 626 SW 2nd 223 (Missouri, 1982), the Missouri Supreme Court reversed a trial court's determination that the law was unconstitutional when it was used in an ex-parte proceeding to prohibit an alleged offender from entering the family home or contacting his children for 15 days. (*Accord Marquette vs. Marquette* 686 P 2nd 990 Oklahoma Court of Appeals, 1984.) In the above noted cases, even though constitutionality of the statute was upheld, the court decisions clearly indicated that they remained troubled by the potential such laws had to limit due process rights of an alleged offender to exceedingly important aspects of his life: his home and often his children. As a result, the constitutionality of such laws still is open to question and remains a fruitful area for discussion in numerous law review articles.[1]

Although typically the application of these laws is upheld when taken to a state's Supreme Court, they have little immediate relevance to any particular victim. She may confront a hostile judge who knows that an appeal of a denial, a preliminary injunction, or a TRO is unlikely. Under such circumstances, it has been noted that judges have "ignored" the availability of TROs and in one state even actively lobbied to have the law repealed (Lerman, 1984). Similarly, the less then ringing endorsement of such orders given by the Administrative Judge of the New York City Family Court demonstrates that victims and their advocates will continue to encounter difficulty in having these orders routinely issued.

Second, as a practical matter, the process of obtaining an injunctive order may be both initiated and pursued by the victim. She often faces seemingly arcane procedural requirements and indifference or even hostility of court personnel and/or the judiciary (Goolkasian, 1986; Waits, 1985).

Third, to be truly effective and enforced as a matter of course by the police, police departments should obtain copies or have a readily available reliable source of the terms of the order. Although the victim might receive a copy, it may not be available during a dispute, and the police might legitimately worry that they are exceeding its terms or the order might have expired, thereby exposing them to charges of false arrest. For this reason, the best system requires court clerks to actually notify police departments. Few such systems exist, or if so, are not kept current. Such computerized systems suffer from budgetary pressures and overall neglect. Significant information gaps occur as a result of these systemic failures, the indifference of court personnel, and/or the inability or unwillingness of the police to monitor such orders.

Fourth, there are real intrinsic limits to the efficacy of any injunctive orders. Hard-core recidivists have repeatedly proven that they are not deterred by prospects of arrest. They are unlikely to stop merely because of another piece of paper that they may choose not to read. The only effective method of stopping these people is for a prosecutor to determine that a felony prosecution is warranted followed by conviction and incapacitation.

Fifth, there is no uniformity of statutes or policies in granting protective orders. Availability of protective orders in any particular case may be limited by statutory restrictions that significantly restrict their use.

- Life-styles of the victim/offender often deny the capability of granting an order. Three states do not allow orders to be issued to former spouses; 13 do not for people who have never been formally married even if "intimates;" and two states, Texas and West Virginia, suspend the availability of protective orders when a divorce or separation action is pending (Finn, 1989).
- Limits have been placed on the type of past conduct that may be used to justify imposition of a restraint. Nine states require proof of actual physical abuse and refuse to grant protective orders in cases of threats or intimidation.
- Further limitations have often been administratively placed upon ex-parte TROs—arguably the most important form of protective order given strong

potential for immediate violence. These limitations reflect the judiciary's ambivalence toward the use of what they see as an extraordinary remedy.

- Numerous procedural limitations exist in many states such as filing fees (which may however be waived at the discretion of the judge) or an inability of a victim to obtain an emergency nighttime or weekend order (Finn, 1989).

In addition to the above limitations on use of all protective orders, there are several additional reasons why divorce-related protective orders have not been used as widely as possible. By their nature, marital orders are limited to cases involving formal marriage, not alternative life-styles. Even in the former case, many states require an aggrieved spouse to initiate divorce proceedings to give the court jurisdiction. In addition, the entire no-fault divorce movement and the pressure of high caseloads encourages court personnel and the judiciary to try to limit these clearly adversarial actions. Finally, the judiciary is aware that a party in a divorce may be motivated to improperly influence custody or property allocation disputes by falsely alleging domestic violence. Allegedly due to the fear of this occurrence, such orders are not often immediately granted or granted ex-parte for only a short period. While certainly legally justifiable, this sets significant roadblocks in their use.

USE AND EFFICACY OF TROS

There is little reported empirical research on the actual use and efficacy of modern TRO statutes. One of the authors participated in developing and analyzing a research program conducted by the Massachusetts Committee on Criminal Justice and funded by the U.S. Bureau of Justice Statistics. This examined the domestic violence practices in eight randomly selected police agencies from October 1986 to December 1986. Despite well-developed laws offering general civil and divorce-related injunctions and official policy to use such orders, police rarely reported having encountered victims protected by injunctive decrees. In fact, out of the 86 domestic violence cases that the officers reported, only 15 protective orders were found in effect.

Even when an officer reported that a victim was protected by a TRO, and a warrantless arrest could therefore be made if its terms were violated, arrests were only made in 3 of the 15 cases or 20%. This was compared to the 11 total arrests of the 171 incidents examined where a TRO had not been issued. In its Final Report, "Police Response to Domestic Violence," the Massachusetts Committee on Criminal Justice (Holmes & Bibel, 1989) stated that since the arrest rate where a court order was in effect was higher than without such an order, this demonstrated the efficacy of protective orders. However, since TROs were present in less than 10% of the cases and even in their presence a rather anemic 20% arrest rate occurred, enthusiasm appears premature.

Furthermore, little empirical research exists on the actual efficacy of the TRO process in stopping abuse. One report suggests that TROs, when used in isolation and without the full commitment by the prosecutors, courts, and police, are not effective. Grau, Fagan, and Wexler (1985) interviewed 270 recipients of TROs. They found that the orders were generally ineffective in either reducing the rate or severity of abuse of serious abusers. Instead, they reported that 60% of the victims studied were abused again regardless of the presence of a restraining order.

This research may, however, mask two markedly different offender sub-populations. A markedly different result occurred when analyzing the behavioral impact of those that were apparently less addicted to an abusive lifestyle. For those with less serious prior histories of family violence or where the abuser was less violent, future acts of domestic violence did decline.

These results are tentative as they measure the effect of an order for only a relatively short time, may relate to the level of understanding and enforcement of TROs in the early 1980s, and are dependent on one measurement of recidivism, the victim's memory (Grau et al., 1985).

CHANGES IN SUBSTANTIVE CRIMINAL LAWS

The second major change in domestic violence related statutes has been the enactment of substantive changes to states' criminal laws. As discussed earlier, many states have amended their statutes to allow a protective order to be enforced by criminal law type. In addition, there has been the enactment in eight states of domestic violence statutes that create a separate criminal offense of domestic or family violence.[2]

At first glance, domestic violence laws may appear superfluous since every state has long had laws prohibiting assault and battery. However, a domestic violence specific statute has several key advantages.

First, it directs law enforcement to the elements of a crime specific to domestic violence, not the generalized laws of assault and battery. This is important since some activities such as harassment, intentional infliction of emotional distress, or threats other than the threat of assault, are difficult to prosecute under the rubric of general assault and battery statutes. The existence of one centralized statute focusing on domestic violence should focus attention to achieve a more active police response. This may occur either because of police officers' enhanced knowledge of the law as applied to domestic violence, or more obliquely a recognition of their increased exposure to civil liability if they knowingly fail to enforce a specific statute.

Second, as discussed earlier, statutes allowing warrantless misdemeanor arrests usually have procedural requirements that may markedly limit their use, for example, strict time limits between the event and the arrest and/or requirements of evidence of visible injury. Creating a new statute gives the legislature a chance to break free from such restrictions.

Third, a domestic violence specific crime makes it far easier for the state to retain better records of the occurrence of reported domestic violence incidents and their case disposition. When such cases are lumped into the generic category of "assault and battery," it is difficult for outside observers to determine with any degree of accuracy whether spousal abuse cases are prosecuted with the same vigor as known assault cases involving unrelated parties.

Fourth, because a domestic violence assault violation is a more specific offense, courts imposing sentences may be more influenced by legislative intent to mete out appropriate punishments. The standard criminal sentences of fines, probation, and/or jail may need to be implemented in domestic violence cases. While it is difficult to prove, the judiciary may use more innovative sentences, such as imposing injunction-like conditions upon release from jail, continuing threats of deferred prosecution, and forced assignment to counseling programs. While these sentences were available in the past and might be undertaken at the initiative of an individual court, they are not intuitively obvious for a sentencing judge rapidly reviewing a plea bargain on a generalized assault charge.

While such statutes clearly have the potential for a widespread effect upon the criminal justice system, evidence is unclear as to how much impact they have had. The U.S. Commission of Civil Rights in its 1978 report, entitled *Battered Women: Issues of Public Policy*, indicated that many judges were then questioning the constitutionality of these statutes on the grounds that they tended to create unwarranted distinctions based on sex and/or marital status. The report also noted, without specific support, that where judges did try to implement the laws aggressively, a case backlog quickly appeared.

While no large-scale empirical study has yet been conducted to analyze the specific impact of such statutes, one study did find that prosecutors were using the statute for charging purposes (Quarm & Schwartz, 1983). As discussed in Chapter 5, the Ohio Domestic Violence Law was widely used after its passage. However, sentencing was undoubtedly lenient and did not appear to reflect statutory preferences for innovation. Since this study was conducted a short time after enactment of the statute, this may reflect the traditional sentencing rather than the new patterns.

CHANGES IN PROSECUTOR'S OPERATIONS

The third category of change being implemented is organizational efforts to reduce the high rates of victim/prosecutor case attrition, adoption of methods to streamline case processing, and attempts to make prosecutors more responsive to victim needs.

Victim Support and Victim Advocate Programs

A concerted federally funded effort to establish a victim-witness support or victim advocates program in prosecutors' offices has been attempted. This was originally tried under sponsorship of an LEAA-funded project (Lerman, 1981). As this was recognized to be a severe problem, such a program was expressly designed to decrease case attrition.

This type of concerted program has the advantage of sensitizing prosecutors to the problems of prosecuting domestic assaults. The concept of a knowledgeable victim advocate also is innovative and may provide critically needed support to a woman who, with relatively few resources, has to confront an indifferent bureaucracy. Finally, such advocates are expected to explain to the woman the availability of shelters, prior restraints, and the services of other social welfare agencies. Lack of knowledge of such services undoubtedly led to many past victim-initiated dismissals.

Such a program may have certain undesirable effects if the organization measures success of a program in terms of the amount of case attrition as opposed to other more victim-centered measurements. Satisfaction with the criminal justice process or the cessation of battering, a concept originally victim oriented, can easily be subverted to serve overriding organizational goals. For this reason, it has been noted that these programs have the potential for being counterproductive when courts try to commit victims to the prosecution process and define success by their own vested interests (Ford & Burke, 1987). Prosecutorial organizations, faced with high caseloads and an increasing backlog, find their interests best served by having fewer total cases but a higher percentage of convictions. This, of course, tends to conflict with the desires of victims to have easy access to a judicial system staffed with helpful, but not dominating, personnel.

The possible results of the role conflict of "victim advocates" is the perpetuation of victim-staff misunderstandings: "Look what we've tried to do without any success or gratitude;" or "They don't understand me and my family and are trying to run my life." Ultimately, a system that strictly measures success in terms of reduced case attrition may act to lessen victim access to justice by deterring them from pursuing otherwise available alternatives. Further research should be conducted to determine if this concern is theoretical or real.

No-Drop Policies

The final, and perhaps most extreme, organizational change has been to impose restrictions on victims that effectively prevents them from freely dropping charges, that is, a "no-drop policy" (Lerman, 1981). This compels the victim to serve as a witness to a crime. She, rather than a complainant responsible for case prosecution, can be subpoenaed if recalcitrant. Simultaneously, there are usually strict limitations to prosecutorial discretion to drop charges except for demonstrated failure of evidentiary support.

LEAA-funded demonstration programs in Cleveland, Los Angeles, Miami, Santa Barbara, Seattle, and Westchester County, New York, have all adopted policies clearly stating that domestic violence will be punished and to varying degrees reduced the victims and prosecutor's ability to drop charges (Lerman, 1981). Such "no-drop" policies have been implemented in a number of jurisdictions.

Five reasons are advanced for this policy. First, domestic violence should be considered as a crime against the public order of the state not just the individual victim whose interests could be protected in a civil action or by protective order. Second, limiting discretion alleviates the problems of relying on largely unsympathetic court personnel by forcing them to justify dismissals only by insufficiency of available evidence. Third, from an organizational perspective, it limits unproductive dropped cases, thereby increasing rates of clearance through convictions. Fourth, such a system has less potential for intimidation or violence against the victim because the decision to continue prosecution is not up to her. Finally, a higher level of specific and general deterrence is prophesied since the probability of a conviction is greatly increased.

In analyzing the policy, it may constitute the judicial equivalence of a "mandatory arrest" policy. Victim autonomy is restricted in the "higher" interest of specific or general deterrence of offenders or a mandate to achieve retribution for an injury suffered. It is also noteworthy that this tactic was previously attempted, although not on any systematic basis. In the late 1800s, the last period of high criminal justice involvement in domestic violence, some courts did sporadically force victims to continue prosecution or risk contempt of court (Pleck, 1989).

While a policy of limited victim and prosecutor discretion certainly has some merit in the context of the pressures placed upon domestic violence victims to dismiss cases, it appears operationally impractical and unwarranted. We base this conclusion on six arguments. First, advocates of this type of program need to focus upon the limited available court resources presently existent. If it is assumed that such resources will not increase merely because a new policy mandating prosecution of one specific class of crimes is adopted, then any increase in time demand from this type of crime must be offset by a diminished capacity of the organization to perform other tasks. Limiting prosecutorial discretion may be justifiable given past tendencies of many bureaucracies to use any vehicle to eliminate such cases (and to a lesser extent to challenge the system). However, it is difficult to persuasively argue that a district attorney should not prosecute, and a court should not hear, a contested criminal case merely in order to try a misdemeanor domestic violence case where a victim does not want prosecution. We believe that the displacement of resources attendant to such a policy should be expressly justified in terms of forcing proponents to explicitly state what tasks now being performed by courts should be foregone in order to implement a no-drop policy.

Second, if victims do not support prosecution or are unconvincing witnesses, it is unlikely that many additional defendants would ever be convicted despite the increase in committed scarce resources.

Third, this policy ignores the complex nature of victims' decisions to desist prosecution. As noted earlier, a victim may drop charges after she has been successful in achieving her primary goal of exercising increased power in a continuing relationship with the offender, at least to the extent of deterring future physical abuse. The failure to allow her to use this power resource may in fact erode the utility of a prosecution. It has been noted that a victim may be safest if she retains the power to drop charges at her discretion. This gives her the ability to manipulate the system to work toward her ends with the threat of continued prosecution as a "victim power resource" (Ford, 1984). The paradox that Ford noted is that she may be safer if she can drop charges but less safe if she actually does decide to drop the charge (Ford, 1984).

Fourth, a no-drop policy may deter victims from reporting crimes. They may gradually become aware that when they do so, they lose control of the process. This loss of control is the antithesis to the views of most feminists. Those advocating this type of control are probably unaware that they may be responding more to the bureaucratic concerns of the largely unsympathetic police and prosecutor, that is, the "fickle victim," than the desires of most victims.

Fifth, such a policy, if coupled with a victim advocacy program, would potentially create a clear conflict of interests between the victim, who might not be interested in pursuing a charge, and the victim advocate whose task it is to process the case. Ultimately, this may cause the victim to lose trust and therefore be less communicative with her nominal "advocate."

Finally, it is incumbent on proponents of such an extreme measure to determine if less disruptive measures would accomplish the same goal. Specifically, a long-term training program to sensitize court personnel, funding of a well-staffed advocacy program, and active efforts to train victims on the judicial process and their rights may all serve the purpose of reducing case attrition without the arbitrary imposition of a "no-drop" policy.

Other Organizational Changes

Other changes in prosecutors' offices have included providing specialized domestic violence training to sensitize the staff to victim needs, and the development of discrimination materials written by qualified professionals to provide victims with written materials on available legal and shelter assistance. These carefully explain the availability of temporary restraining orders pending trial. Finally, some jurisdictions such as Santa Barbara, California, have developed integrated teams of police, prosecutors, and social workers under federal demonstration grants. They have facilitated coordination between the police departments and prosecutors.

To date, little research has been conducted that has empirically evaluated whether any efforts to organizationally improve prosecutorial performance have led to diminished case attrition, or any other more victim-oriented measurement of success. There is currently a NIJ-funded field experiment on prosecution being conducted in Indianapolis. However, the results of this research have not yet been released.

Existing studies of the impact of individual programs suggest that change may be forthcoming. One study of the pilot program in Westchester County, New York, observed that 82% of the charges in the domestic violence prosecution unit were followed through by victims. Of those charges, more than 94% of the defendants were convicted. However, the same study noted that other programs reported earlier impressive changes in terms of fewer voluntary dismissals and more domestic violence offenders held ultimately accountable. These attributes disappeared when organizational and personnel changes were made (Pirro, 1982). Clearly, a commitment must be sustained to ensure that the prosecutor's office doesn't treat this as merely another public relations "cause" with short-term goals. They may subsequently fail to commit essential resources for a lengthy period of time. Given the exigencies of budgetary dilemmas currently facing most state governments, this is likely to be an acute problem.

DIVERSION AND INNOVATIONS IN SENTENCING

Many prosecutors and members of the judiciary have gradually begun to recognize that one of the primary reasons why the criminal justice system has been ineffective in responding to domestic violence has been the relative inflexibility of treatment modalities for ending violent outbursts. Two different models of diversion from the system adopting markedly different premises have been developed: mediation of disputes and counseling by court mandate as a condition for pretrail diversion or as part of sentencing subsequent to a guilty plea or trial verdict.

"Sponsored" Mediation Programs

Formal mediation of interpersonal disputes (in contrast to informal efforts by police and others to settle a dispute in the residence of the parties) uses the services of a skilled intermediary. Parties are shown how to resolve serious differences without recourse to violent or inappropriate behavior. The mediator does not have the authority to mandate any particular settlement, and instead typically seeks to develop a process for solving disputes rationally and nonviolently.

Mediation efforts to contain domestic violence have been developed from two perspectives. At least several hundred crisis intervention centers nationwide have been set up to attempt to diffuse many different kinds of interpersonal disputes, including domestic violence. These efforts, although a vital component of society's response to domestic violence, are not covered in this book. A detailed study of such programs is contained in *Domestic Violence Mediation Demands Careful Screening* by L. Ray (1982).

A second mediation source, of more relevance to this book, has been the use of pre-trial mediation sponsored by the prosecutor's office. These programs may be run by the prosecutorial or judicial staff or may be contracted out to use the services of local crisis management agencies.[3]

The theory behind the use of mediation as a diversionary program is that the abuser, and even at times the abused party, may deny the essential criminality of spouse abuse conduct. Mediation finesses the need for such a determination. The process and techniques for settling conflicts without violence are taught to both offender and victim. This has been favored by some as a method of circumventing an impersonal court system that discriminates against the needs of women. It further serves as a method of educating both parties about their legal rights and responsibilities.

Types of Mediation Programs

Formal mediation programs are extraordinarily varied in nature. The better programs use a structured framework that seeks to teach long-term dispute resolution within the societally acceptable nonviolent context. Some programs have even included initial direct sessions with a mediator and a surrogate or advocate for the "adversary." During the course of the mediation, techniques are taught for constructive venting of anger by both parties. Similarly, the victim is given guidance about her rights and available support systems for victims of battering.

In other programs, sessions between the spouses are preceded by individual counseling of both the accused offender and the victim. This lessens the immediate trauma of the incident, allows a careful evaluation of the parties' commitment to mediation, begins teaching each party their rights and responsibilities, and may provide requisite psychological counseling. To memorialize the process and reinforce the commitment to change, a formal signed mediation agreement is usually prepared setting forth mutually agreed upon goals.

Still other programs only accept couples where the assailant has conditionally admitted that he or she did assault the victim. This type of mediation begins to resemble a conditional sentencing program inconsistent with the nonjudgmental tenets of mediation.

Enforcement of this agreement and future nonviolence should be handled by careful case monitoring. The program should be coupled with prosecutorial commitments that if such interviews or victims' reports disclose violation of the mediation agreement, a suspended prosecution will be reinstated for both the original and any new acts of violence. Lerman (1982) provided a good analysis of the components of such a program. In her article, she also details the many problems and limitations attendant to this type of diversion.

Does Mediation Reduce Violence?

Although there is little direct empirical evidence, preliminary studies suggest that alternate programs such as mediation provide approximately equal reductions in the rate of recidivism compared to traditional court sentencing. Bethel and Singer (1981-1982) found the District of Columbia's mediation service effective in reducing future violence and considered fair by both parties (Cook, Roehl, & Sheppard, 1980; Davis, Tichane, & Grayson, 1980; Feldstiner & Williams, 1980; and studies for the Vera Institute and the Victim Services Agency).

Of course, some authors believe it is inappropriate to compare recidivism rates with a criminal justice system "known to avoid wife abuse cases." These authors, often quite hostile to most court-sponsored diversion programs, including mediation, assert that such comparisons are irrelevant. They believe the real comparison should be to the outcome attainable in a nonsexist legal system (Stallone, 1984). Despite the merit of this critique—we should after all aim for the *best* response possible—comparisons between real world alternatives do remain the best indicators of what is a useful policy. This being the case, it is essential to carefully consider the advantages and disadvantages of mediation.

ADVANTAGES OF MEDIATION

From this perspective, mediation does have several significant advantages. Despite its intensive time commitments for counselors and mediators, most cases do not require much of the far scarcer judicial resources. Hence it may be considered expedient to an overburdened system facing "gridlock" at the trial court level. Empirical studies have shown that participants of effective programs view the process as being fair and generally rate it more favorably than the vagaries of the traditional, overworked, and cynical court system (Bethel & Singer, 1982; Cook, Roehl, & Sheppard, 1980; Davis, Tichane, Grayson, 1986; Smith, 1983).

DISADVANTAGES OF MEDIATION

Mediation shares some of the basic tenets of the "conciliatory" style of policing. Specifically, it does not seek to legally fix blame upon either party. As a result, it doesn't distinguish between the actions of the victim and the aggressor. Many batterers appear able to deny the essential criminality of their actions without a strong criminal justice system punishing the violent conduct. It is possible that by implying that neither party is solely to blame, mediation will allow or even encourage an assailant to view his conduct as not being expressly wrong, but merely a product of a "bad" relationship partially the fault of "provocations" by the woman.

If inappropriately used, the result could be the continued "subjugation" of a woman because the criminal acts of violence are treated merely as a result of the "dysfunctional" family unit. See especially Lisa Lerman (1984) for this line of argument. Hence mediation should best be reserved to less serious cases of threats of assault, low-level acts of violence, or the "battling spouses" paradigm.

In contrast, cases of repeated series assaults should normally be treated as a crime. This dichotomy should exist both for the necessary goal of punishing violent antisocial behavior and because available evidence suggests that offenders who have already committed repeated acts of serious abuse are less likely to benefit from such programs by changing behavior (Bethel & Singer, 1982). This may create problems for the intake/selection of such programs given the lack of agreement over the definition of "severe" abuse. Severe abuse disqualifying a couple might, for example, include one incident involving injuries requiring hospitalization or involving use of a weapon. Alternatively, participation by a couple with a long-recorded history of prior incidents might be eliminated.

In some jurisdictions, misdemeanor domestic assaults continued by a particular offender result in the recategorization of such crime to a *felony*, hence subjecting the assailant to the potential of far more severe punishment. If there is a significant chance of recidivism in a jurisdiction with this type of domestic violence statute, the prosecution will not only have given up the chance to prosecute for one particular act of violence, but also the opportunity to more rapidly invoke laws needed to deter habitual offenders.

Requirements placed upon the conduct of both parties also limit the appropriate use of mediation. Obviously, since active participation is required, a mediation program cannot be effective where the couple has become estranged or where either party does not seek a reconciliation (Greenstein, 1982). Similarly, it should not be used, even if both parties are willing to try, if one party is unable to represent his or her interests. Should the proposed mediator believe that temperament, past traumatic shock, or strongly ingrained beliefs in a master-subordinate relationship is present, an adversarial process with a victim advocate should be far superior (Lerman, 1984).

Mediation programs also require a continued commitment of state and local funding. Too often, "demonstration projects," announced with great fanfare by federal and state funding agencies, are started, proven initially effective, and continued for a time. However, in subsequent periods of budgetary austerity, the push for efficiency in terms that are easily quantifiable may become overwhelming. Mediation programs are uniquely vulnerable to such delusion as they are highly dependent upon the qualifications and time commitments of the mediators. Degradations of results may easily occur if quantifiable measures of efficiency, such as cases per mediator, become the litmus test of efficacy. Unfortunately, accountability of mediation systems is low due to the necessary secrecy of most mediation efforts. Therefore, systemic decay caused by insufficient funding or a decline in organizational commitment may not immediately be realized (Pirro, 1982).

Such decay may have unfortunate results even beyond missing an opportunity to effectively intervene. Mediation, even if ineffective at stopping violence, increases the likelihood of the family staying together, at least during the period of the mediation. It is known that intimacy of contact increases the potential for conflicts. If the mediation is unsuccessful at limiting the assailant's potential for violence, there is a real probability that it may leave the victim worse off than if the case was not diverted from the criminal justice system.

One research paper by Smith (1983) did show that 36% of victims reported more violence after mediation, and 41% had increased fears of revenge. Of course this study did not answer what percentage of these women would have reported such results without mediation, nor could it reflect the potential for conflict management of all the various forms of mediation.

Finally, implicit in mediation is the assumption that the parties should be able to compromise their disparate interests to maintain a previously dysfunctional relationship. The implied primary goal of maintenance of a family unit has been directly challenged by many feminists who argue that violence abatement should take precedence. They argue that mediation is an attempt to pacify feminists without changing the underlying neglect of women's legitimate interests (Stallone, 1984). Introducing the potentially conflicting goal of family maintenance might in turn dilute the importance of ending violence.

Similarly, many feminists fear that in the zeal to reach a mutually satisfactory accommodation, women may be pressured into abstaining from "aggressive" or "provocative" behavior thus achieving the abuser's goal of dominating a relationship without the necessity of resorting to violence. For example, how would a mediator react to such "provocative behavior" as the woman failing to do certain household chores adequately in the eyes of the batterer? Such a precipitator is known to be the immediate trigger of most acts of violence in the family. Should the mediator tell the woman that she must be willing to do these chores to her husband's specifications to avoid a beating? Placed in this focus, it is the inability of the man to resolve the inevitable familial conflicts without resorting to violence that should be addressed. In an especially stinging critique of the entire theoretical basis and application of mediation, Stallone states that mediation shelters nurture sexism and hence should be eliminated in most cases. She believes that in the guise of keeping the family together, the woman's autonomy is restricted, and the criminal court is unable to prevent violence.

Counseling Programs

Assumptions and Use of Counseling Programs for Batterers

Counseling programs rely upon an assumption that character traits or inappropriate learned behavior patterns favoring violence lead to recurrent violent explosions. They believe violence may be altered through intervention of skilled counselors. Such counseling ideally would begin almost immediately after a violent episode when the offender feels most remorseful and receptive to suggestions for change. Although counseling and mediation share the distinction of being programs to divert offenders from the criminal justice system, they present some real distinctions.

Counseling programs have one key advantage over mediation. The focus of counseling is firmly upon inappropriate actions of the offender and the necessity of modifying this behavior. As a result, it may more predictably lead the offender to realize that he has acted inappropriately and needs to change his behavior as opposed to a "conflict resolution" model.

Programs for clinical assistance to domestic violence batterers have been in existence since the mid-1970s. By 1986, one author estimated that such programs increased from virtually none in 1975 to more than 100 different operations (Goolkasian, 1986). One recent trend has been the direct involvement of the criminal justice system in increasing the flow of client referrals from judicial proceedings.

By the mid-1980s, it was estimated that one-third of all offenders that were being seen by counselors came from court referrals (Goolkasian, 1986). The increasing relative importance of court referrals has been a change in direction for many programs. If pressed, most mental health practitioners would state that profound personality changes needed to eliminate deeply ingrained violent tendencies are most effective if the client has recognized his deviance and voluntarily chooses counseling. Although this may be true, many are not strong willed enough to take or at least complete independent corrective action. This is especially true of batterers, who as a class, have often been described as "denying the essential deviance of their acts" and therefore will not often seek treatment voluntarily. Instead, they appear to need to be prodded by fear of court sanctions to enroll and complete counseling programs.

Prosecutorial and court involvement may be a diversion of the suspect prior to trial or as a component of his sentence. Diversion prior to trial has been done informally by prosecutors, formally through administrative procedures as in the federally funded demonstration projects noted earlier or even by statute, as in Arizona, California, and Wisconsin. In addition, court-mandated counseling is rapidly growing as a part of sentencing or as a condition of a plea bargain.

Program Characteristics

Suspension of prosecution is critical to diversionary use of counseling if the offender agrees to counseling and attends required sessions. If a counseling program is indeed deemed to be successful for a particular offender, then after an established time period, such as six months or a year and/or completion of a counseling program, the original suspended prosecution is dropped, and records of the original offense are destroyed or filed. Alternatively, if the offender leaves counseling, or recidivates, the prosecutor is theoretically committed to prosecuting both the original and any subsequent offenses.

Access to batterer programs should be restricted to those most likely to benefit. Lerman (1981) reported that some programs use formal contracts to match offender commitments to change their behavior and attend counseling sessions with an agreement from the prosecution regarding his future actions. Within limits, such agreements may be tailor made to the offender's individual needs. For example, they may contain intermediate goals such as cessation of substance abuse and/or prevention of any further contact with the victim until counseling has been completed. Naturally the long-term goal of all such programs is to rehabilitate the offender to end his propensity for violent outbursts.

Effective programs are usually interdisciplinary. Screening of the cases might be handled by the prosecutor's office with assistance of domestic violence specialists. The counseling itself is usually handled by community-based mental health professionals. Subsequent case tracking to monitor for relapses is done by experienced probation officers.

When counseling is used for pretrail diversion, it should be considered differently than counseling imposed as a form of sentence. In the former case, the prosecutor must be cognizant of the responsibility to protect the defendant's constitutional rights, including making certain that he knows that charges will be reinstated if the offender quits the counseling program.

Advantages of Counseling

There are several distinct advantages of court-sponsored counseling, especially as a diversion from the criminal justice system. It finesses the greatest weakness of the system: its inability to prevent victims or prosecutors from dismissing charges. By selective use of counseling as a diversion, the finite available resources may be more effectively focused upon cases where recidivism occurs or the potential for serious continued violence appears great.

Pretrail diversion to counseling is also appropriate for the many instances where the preferred judicial sentence would be probation coupled with such a program. In these cases, the ideal result is to accomplish this quickly without incurring heavy transactional costs to the judicial system, or the necessity of labeling the offender as a convicted miscreant and hence risking secondary deviance. As noted earlier, the period immediately after the battering incident may see the defendant most amenable to behavioral change. Avoiding long court proceedings may actually serve to increase the immediacy of the counseling and its ultimate chance of success.

Limitations of Counseling

Such programs have certain severe limitations. Administration of counseling programs is difficult. Counseling, other than on a group basis, is time intensive and expensive to an overloaded system. The costs of counseling itself are but one component of the total rehabilitation cost. Case monitoring and tracking is exceedingly important. If an offender loses contact with the criminal justice system, it would be relatively easy to push the limits of the program and gain little real benefit. For this reason, costs of handling indigent offenders far exceed those for voluntary dismissal cases where the prosecutor merely agrees to a negotiated plea followed by minimally supervised probation.

This conflict over scarce resources is clearly understood by some feminists who have argued that more funds have been placed upon shelters for battered women rather than counseling for offenders (Stanko, 1989). Morally this position is difficult to refute. The needs of victims of crimes should take precedence over those of an offender; the unfortunate reality is that shelters provide a brief respite from abuse, "harden the target," and sometimes lead a woman from an inherently destructive relationship. However, if the offender is not rehabilitated, violence is likely to flare again with that woman or possibly another victim. For this reason, allocation of resources to offender counseling, if successful, may prove to be even more effective than shelters and in any event, a good complement to such efforts. However, for cost reasons alone, it is acknowledged that it is unlikely that counseling will ever be the primary method of treating domestic violence occurrences.

Evaluation of Counseling Programs

A significant amount of research has been conducted to evaluate the success of counseling programs. One easily measured criterion is the short-term goal of program completion. It does appear that court-mandated programs have higher rates of completion than those servicing voluntary participants. Rates for program completion may be different because of the documented ability of offenders to deny the irrational and criminal nature of their conduct. Without compulsion, batterers may enter a program during the "honeymoon" or "remorseful stage" of a typical domestic violence cycle. When this mood changes the "voluntary" offender may more quickly drop out (Coates & Leong, 1980; Farrington, 1980; Green, 1984).

All of the foregoing studies explore conditions leading to offenders exiting programs. One study of a program in Miami found that only 17 out of 260 offender participants in a court-mandated program terminated the program (Pirog-Good & Stets, 1986). These authors also conducted a national survey and estimated that there was at least 60% program completion for entrants to mandatory counseling programs. *Accord* Gondolf (1984), who reported a 52% completion rate for court-mandated programs.

The longer term, and far more significant goal, is to rehabilitate the offender to remove the inappropriate orientation of resorting to violence. After all, it is hardly a resounding success if an offender continues to engage in violence despite having completed the counseling program.

In addition to being a measure of short-term success, program completion may provide a reasonably good indicator of prospects for future recidivism. Studies that have assessed the frequency of recurring violence as indicia of program effectiveness have shown different rates of recidivism for program completers versus those that have quit the program. Among program completers, reported rates of recidivism have varied considerably in different studies. Depending on whether success is defined as the complete cessation of violence versus a reduction in frequency or severity of violence, rates of recidivism have ranged from a low of 2% (Dutton, 1986) to 9% as reported by Lerman (1981), 12% (Pirog-Good & Stets, 1986); 15% (Helpern, 1984); 28% (Hamberger & Hastings, 1986); to as high as 39% (Gondolf, 1984).

The variability in reported recidivism may be an artifact of the small sample sizes in the studies, varying sampling techniques used, the different measures of recidivism, and the fact that much of the evaluative research has been written by people responsible for program implementation, a clear conflict of interest. A standardized research protocol, or at least easily replicable standard of measurement does not presently exist. For example, Dutton (1987) freely acknowledged that the subjects in his 1986 study were batterers whose participation and treatment was determined in part by their willingness to participate in the treatment program (Dutton, 1987). The extremely low recidivism rate of 2% obtained in his study may therefore be partially due to the self-selection of a group likely to be positively impacted by counseling. Recidivism data in other studies originated in a national survey of violence abatement programs (Pirog-Good & Stets, 1986) or estimates of recurrence obtained from victims, batterers, and police reports. Thus variability in reported recidivism rates may not only reflect probable success/failure rates of various programs, but also the variance in treatment selection criteria and the sources of recidivism data.

As a result of such definitional issues, there is no large-scale empirical research yet available to compare recidivism rates in the same program for program completers versus noncompleters. However, some smaller-scale studies that compared recidivism of these two groups have shown differences. Dutton (1986) and Hamberger and Hastings (1986) found significantly lower rates of recidivism among completers as contrasted with studies of Gondolf (1984), Halpern (1984), and Hawkins and Beauvais (1985), where no significant differences were found between these groups for recidivism rates.

In addition, most research merely reports the possible impact of a type of change judged in isolation. This, of course, is merely an abstract of reality where changes are constantly being proposed and adopted. Multivariate empirical research that factors together the impact of different types of changes in the criminal justice response to domestic violence has just begun to be conducted.

There is, however, at least some indication that, in addition to its own direct segregable impact upon recidivism, court-mandated counseling may have an indirect role mediating upon the success of other efforts to deter domestic violence. A linkage may exist between the use of arrest sanctions and rehabilitation through counseling. Dutton and Strachan (1987) found an apparent contradiction in the literature in recidivism after arrest. They found studies with an arrest affect upon recidivism basically used short-term measurements of success such as six months for Sherman and Berk (1984). However, they found that recidivism increased considerably, almost 40%, 30 months after the arrest when no further criminal justice action or treatments followed the initial arrest compared to only 4% of the group that received counseling. In fact, they found that 84% of the wives of treated men reported no further acts of severe violence directed toward them during the entire 30-month follow-up period. Thus, a great long-term decrease in recidivism appears to occur when arrest is paired with treatment (Dutton, 1986). If this is confirmed in subsequent research, it suggests that arrest by itself may have only a short-term deterrent effect. Dutton believes that long-term reduction in recidivism requires active efforts to rehabilitate the offender. The question raised by these results is whether fear of a future arrest itself deters, or whether instead arrest is merely a vehicle to require the offender to enter counseling or other rehabilitative programs. These then might produce the long-term reduction in recidivism. Dutton's study now needs to be expanded to determine if the arrest component itself has any long-term impact itself, or if the same result would occur if the offender entered a court-mandated program after having been brought in to the criminal justice system via a complaint and summons.

We should also resist considering the category of treatment programs as a monolithic entity. Such programs can and do vary enormously in structure and even in their purpose. Such changes may impact upon the rates of program success. For example, sophistication and size of the program and the type of counseling (group versus individual sessions) intuitively would seem to have the potential to produce different rates of program success. The number of sessions attended and the duration of sessions has already been reported as being such a determinative factor (Gondolf, 1984).

Similarly, the definition of when a program ends for an individual, for example, at a set number of sessions or when psychological testing shows a likelihood of long-term personality/response change may affect success rates. There is no known research reporting such differences although Deschner (1984), Hamberger and Hastings (1986), and Hawkins and Beauvais (1985) all report that the mental health of the abuser at the end of the program appears to be important to long-range prospects for success. Similarly, future studies of the impact of such rehabilitative programs should assess offenders to determine if individual characteristics of the offender, such as age, race, ethnic origin, prior histories of crime, and substance-abuse profile, significantly bear upon the rates of program success.

NOTES

1. See especially Dorothy Quinn (1985); Mutual Orders of Protection in New York State Family Offense Proceedings: A Denial of "Liberty without Due Process of Law supra and Ex Parte Proceedings in Domestic Violence Situations: Alternative Frameworks for Constitutional Scrutiny 9 *Hofstra Law Review* 95 (1980). A shorter representative case note is, "Ex Parte Provision of Adults Abuse Act Ruled Constitutional," *American Journal of Trial Advocacy*, Vol. 6, pp. 197-198 also "Statutory Authority in the Use and Enforcement of Civil Protection Orders Against Domestic Abuse," *supra* provides an excellent overview and analysis not only of the constitutional arguments but also of various capabilities and limitations of protective orders in each of the states where enacted.

2. As of mid-1989, the following states have made various aspects of domestic violence a separate criminal offense: Arkansas (relates to abuse by husbands only), California, Hawaii, North Carolina (covering spouses and persons who have lived "as if married"), and Ohio (but only as to members of the same household related by blood or marriage), parents, children, spouse and persons cohabitating or formerly cohabitating, and Tennessee. Also, a number of states while not specifically adding a domestic violence charge, now cross reference existing assault laws in their new domestic violence statutes. This has apparently been done to emphasize to police and prosecutors that these statutes should be considered in tandem with domestic violence specific laws in appropriate Massachusetts and New Hampshire (these laws include the unusual provision for fines to be paid to victim) and Wisconsin where the court may release an offender to the custody of a third party such as a counseling agent or a probation officer.

3. Although not a diversionary program, on rare occasions mediation has been used as a component of conditional sentencing after the determination of guilt. This, however, is not nearly as common given the difference between the non-value oriented conflict resolution approach of mediation and the determination of culpability implicit in a guilty plea or verdict.

Conclusions

THE STATUS OF CHANGE

It is likely that the relevant criminal justice bureaucracies will probably never like to intervene in cases of domestic assault. Such incidents are likely to be perceived as peripheral to their primary mission, are not intrinsically a pleasant duty, and few, if any, organizational rewards will ever exist for effective performance. Despite this, the criminal justice system as a system remains defensive on the provision of services to battered women. Hence, it is vulnerable to change "directed" by federal agencies, suggested by research, or to political and administrative pressure from the risks of lawsuits or adverse publicity arising from charges of misfeasance by battered women's advocates.

The criminal justice system has made major structural changes to accommodate needs of domestic violence victims. As part of a sweeping change directed by virtually all states, legal impediments to effective police action have largely been removed. Officers may now make warrantless arrests for misdemeanors, for violation of new substantive laws against domestic violence, or, in many states, if they believe the terms of a protective order have been violated.

Despite such capabilities and the frank encouragement of action by state government, actual observable change in "street level" justice has not consistently been attained. This is only partially attributable to the inherent time lag between statutory enactment directing change and its actual implementation. Of perhaps even greater significance is the clear and growing dichotomy between attitudes of the majority of police administrators and the rank and file within their departments. Police administrators have largely joined with academic and professional researchers and advocates of battered women and feminists activists to attempt to expand the role of the criminal justice system. Some do so because of an actual attitudinal change and recognition that past police practices inappropriately ignored a class of victims. Others recognize that the potential for liability awards and further political pressure mandate change even if they do not fully share the ultimate goals. Still others appear to be reacting to the latest trend being promulgated by federal agencies—be it crisis intervention or more recently the use of arrests as a deterrent.

No such attitudinal change has occurred with the police rank and file or their frontline supervisors. With some notable exceptions, concentrated among minority and female officers and those recently trained in domestic violence intervention, such officers still consider the criminal justice response to be largely ineffective and dangerous to themselves. It is not considered a real job and, unlike the case of police administrators, few if any organizational inducements currently exist or have even been proposed to try to motivate this group to perform their job more effectively.

A training program *if well constructed* may change attitudes; however, research does not clearly establish whether such changes will continue long term. In any event, budgetary exigency has led to wholesale abandonment of training programs that already had demonstrated short-term efficacy. For example, it appears that in Massachusetts, the Criminal Justice Training Council that had provided all pre-service and in-service training for police agencies in the Commonwealth of Massachusetts will be closed in June 1990 due to a complete loss of funding. Similarly, Detroit, Michigan, was forced to abandon an innovative training program due to lack of funds. In today's budgetary climate, it is unlikely that many departments will be able to devote the scarce resources for additional training, absent litigation, or political pressure.

Under these circumstances, there is a real question as to whether street-level justice will really change. The rank and file have the demonstrated ability to resist directed change if they disagree with its premises. Despite this, empirical research has clearly shown that some change has occurred. When police administrators insist on a more proactive policy, even in the absence of statutory mandate, an observable increase in arrests has been demonstrated. The challenge is whether such change will continue after the initial period following an order when nonconformance might be termed to be direct disobedience to higher authority.

Change in the structure/operations of the judicial system clearly is, however, not as advanced as in the case of the police. For example, while virtually all states have broadened and systematized the process of issuing protective orders to victims, the actual use of such orders is restricted, and they are simply not being issued by many judges. While innovations in some prosecutors' offices suggest that the abysmal rates of voluntary and directed dismissals might be mitigated, such efforts are not to any degree uniform, are being adopted piecemeal, and are subject to reversal if funding for "demonstration projects" collapses or key personnel leave the organization. In addition, there is a paucity of research to assess if these programs are appropriate. Similarly, while the new domestic violence statutes have increased the possibility of sophisticated charging and sentencing, little empirical research exists that demonstrates that such statutes are actually being effectively used by prosecutors and the judiciary.

Perhaps the only judicial area where change is readily apparent is the expansion and systemization of the use of formal pretrial diversion in the form of prosecutorial sponsored mediation and counseling. These programs are proliferating and may become the dominant method of handling minor acts or threats of domestic violence. This is occurring despite vocal resistance by battered women's advocates who tend to favor an approach based more upon deterrence and the application of punitive sanctions. Despite valid criticisms and important limitations of such actions, we believe that such programs may prove to be the only opportunity to effect offender rehabilitation given the absence of effective police crisis intervention or referrals to other social agencies. These also allow scarce resources to be focused upon the more serious cases of abuse. It is, of course, an open issue as to whether such pretrail diversion methods have been adopted primarily because of their rehabilitative potential or because they serve an organizational need for rapid, low-cost case disposition.

The effect of such differential rates of change is hard to assess. Clearly, the "system" to the extent it ever "uniformly" ignored the needs of victims, has lost this feature. Instead, change has been adopted unsystematically at varying rates even within a particular jurisdiction. To some extent, this ferment is good as it increases the likelihood that innovative approaches to assist victims are tried. Regrettably, however, the result for any particular victim is that it is rare that she will be assisted competently and with sympathy from the initial encounter with the police, through case management with the prosecutor's office, to an ultimate case resolution that seeks to rehabilitate or at a minimum deter an offender. Without this occurring, she may simply find the "mouth of the funnel," that is, the police intake process, to have enlarged but the ultimate capacity of the system to help her at the later stages remains inadequate. Such a result not only increases her frustration, but also constitutes a waste of scarce resources.

THE ATTEMPT TO LIMIT AGENCY DISCRETION

Frustration with the progress of change has rapidly mounted especially in the community of professional service providers who assist female victims and to a lesser extent, with academics and departmental administration. This has been expressed by the willingness of the first two groups to enthusiastically support efforts to limit agency discretion by mandating arrests in the context of policing or by limiting the prosecutor' ability to drop charges.

We share the frustrations that are expressed by these professionals. Clearly, past practices of the police, prosecutors, and the judiciary have abused their discretion, ignored the real needs of a class of victims, and by such conduct serve to perpetuate the cycle of violence. However, for the reasons that we stated in earlier chapters, we think eliminating discretion as a remedy ultimately will prove ill-advised, unlikely to cure the organizational problem it addressed, and likely to impose unexpected burdens on the victim and the agency being so directed.

Instead of the mechanistic approach implied by abandoning discretion and mandating change, we believe that a preferable outcome would be to train officers and prosecutors to use their discretion wisely. This may be done by "presumptive policies" favoring a particular course of action while leaving it still to the official discretion, or by forcing the official to justify nonconforming actions in writing via a uniform case disposition report open to the inspection/oversight of other officials. In addition, all parties, regardless of their ideological position on use of arrests, should work together to increase resources devoted to training police and prosecutors. We do believe that such training, if well developed and reinforced at regular intervals by front line managers, may eventually produce a police response that is more proactive than in the past and far more flexible than the rigidity implied by a mandatory arrest policy.

Finally, although prosecutorial discretion has been abused in the past, we think that the increased potential for frustration of a victim's highly individual needs mitigates against adopting a "no-drop" policy. We again prefer increased use of training on victim needs and their use of discretion. This could and should be combined with more effective use of "victim advocates" and a staff of prosecutors that, at least in larger jurisdictions, are committed full time to processing domestic violence crimes. Under such circumstances, agency discretion should not be the enemy of the needs of battered women but instead an effective resource to help her.

RESEARCH IN THE CHANGE PROCESS

Clearly research results in this area have had a critical impact in framing the policy debates and even the actual provision of services.

On several occasions, we have observed that seminal research projects, although in reality quite limited in research terms, have had an effect in this area far beyond their original scope. They have made the problem of the societal response to domestic violence salient to the public (Garner re Sherman, 1990), and have changed the direction of the preferred outcome (Binder, 1989, re Sherman, 1984; Mayo re Bard, 1990; Sherman, 1989).

The remaining question, however, is whether there are moral and ethical responsibilities of researchers to wait for conclusive results to determine the best policy, thereby avoiding promoting a policy that might actually injure victims or offenders or have unanticipated consequences. Alternately, if a more rigorous intellectual pursuit of knowledge is attempted, will research *ever* have an impact or will it remain the province of academics who as a group must (if honest) admit to enjoying continual internecine warfare on virtually any topic. While we cannot, of course, provide any answer to this debate, we can make the following observations:

Most writing in this field is preliminary in nature. The reports often rely on overgeneralized assumption of agency conduct or are based on small-scale studies conducted many years earlier. In doing so, they risk being based on the premise, perhaps accurate years earlier, that the police, prosecutors, and the judiciary monolithically treat domestic violence with a policy of not too benign neglect. To some extent, this reflects that "conventional wisdom" and research protocols have not yet observed the diversity of responses of today's criminal justice system. In other cases, it reflects a feminist ideological orientation that is best served by *not* acknowleding the changes in the criminal justice system.

For whatever reasons, most proposed changes such as new mandatory arrest policies are treated in isolation as a change from the "classic" pattern of response. Little attempt is made in the literature to integrate the perspective that change has and is rapidly occurring throughout the system. Similarly, scant attention is placed upon the effect of implementation systems and attendant training programs upon observed performance. Therefore, it is difficult if not impossible in many cases to determine whether a perceived effect is inherent in the particular reform being tested, or is an artifact of the implementation or training system of the particular agency.

Similarly, much of the reported research does not focus sufficiently on the complex nature of the interaction between the victims and offender on the one hand and the police and prosecutors on the other. Subtle situational behavioral changes by both sets of actors may markedly change the observed outcome of the intervention. This subtlety is lost when research tends, in our view, to become obsessively focused on one easily quantifiable policy outcome, the decision to arrest, or on one of the various methods of measuring recidivism. In stating this, it is acknowledged that there is a need to create a simplified model to conduct and report research; however, the limitations on the internal and external validity of such projects should be explicitly stated and policy preferences, if given, should be understood as being based upon incomplete knowledge.

Finally, we share the observations of Ohlin and Tonry (1989) that much of the domestic violence and criminal justice research on the subject has not really fully absorbed and integrated the other's body of knowledge. This has, on occasion, led family violence researchers to propose "solutions" to the problem of changing the criminal justice system that those more familiar with police literature might recognize as being naive, or at least unworkable without a detailed implementation plan, and a poor understanding of the resources and support needed to obtain attitudinal and behavioral change within an organization. Similarly, criminal justice researchers studying this area often have not shown sufficient understanding or sensitivity to their inherent assumptions regarding the causation and treatment of domestic violence, the needs of its victims, and the best method of treating domestic violence. As a result, policy prescriptions that they propose may solve specific problems of organizations but lack the capability of effectively intervening in the domestic violence cycle.

References

Balos, B., & Trotsky, I. (1988). Enforcement of the domestic abuse act in Minnesota: A preliminary study. *Law and Inequality, 6,* 83-125.

Bannon, J. (1974). *Social conflict assaults: Detroit, Michigan.* Unpublished report for the Detroit Police Department and the Foundation.

Bannon, J. (1975, August). *Law enforcement problems with intra family violence.* Speech delivered to the American Bar Association, Montreal, Canada.

Barancik, J. I., et al. (1983). Northeastern Ohio Trauma Study. I. Magnitude of the problem. *American Journal of Public Health, 73,* 746-751.

Bard, M. (1973). *Training police in family crisis intervention.* Washington, DC: U.S. Government Printing Office.

Bard, M., & Zacker, J. (1974). Assualtiveness and alcohol use in family disputes. *Criminology, 12,* 281-92.

Bassett, S. (1980). *Battered rich.* Port Washington, NY: Ashley Books.

Bayley, D. H. (1986). The tactical choices of police patrol officers. *Journal of Criminal Justice, 14,* 329-348.

Bell, D. (1984). The police responses to domestic violence: A replication study. *Police Studies, 7,* 136-43.

Berk, R. A., Berk, S. F., Loseke, D. R., & Rauma, D. (1983). Mutual combat and other family violence myths. In D. Finkelhor, R. J. Gelles, G. T. Hotaling, & M. S. Straus (eds.) *The dark side of families.* (pp. 197-212). Beverly Hills, CA: Sage.

Berk, R. A., Berk, S. F., Newton, P. J., & Loseke, D. R. (1984). Cops on call: Summoning the police to the scene of spousal violence. *Law and Society Review, 18*(3), 479-498.

Berk, S. F., & Loseke, D. R. (1980-1981). "Handling" family violence: Situational determinants of police arrests in domestic disturbances. *Law and Society Review, 15*(2), 317-346.

Berk, R., & Newton, P. (1985). Does arrest deter wife battery? An effort to replicate the findings of the Minneapolis spouse abuse experiment. *American Sociological Review, 50,* 253-262.

Bethel, C. A., & Singer, L. R. (1981-1982). Mediation: A new remedy for causes of domestic violence. *Vermont Law Review, 6,*2 and 7,1.

Binder, A., & Meeker, J. (1988). Experiments as reforms. *Journal of Criminal Justice, 16,* 347-358.

Binney, V., Harkell, G., & Nixon, J. (1985). Refuges and housing for battered women. In J. Pahl (Ed.), *Private violence and public policy.* Boston, MA: Routledge & Kegan Paul.

Bittner, E. (1967). The police on skid row: A study of peace keeping. *American Sociological Review, 32,* 699-715.

Bittner, E. (1974). Florence Nightingale in pursuit of Willie Sutton: A theory of the police. In H. Jacob (Ed.), *The potential for reform of criminal justice.* Beverly Hills, CA: Sage.

Black, D. (1976). *The behavior of law.* New York: Academic Press.

Black, D. (1980). *The manners and customs of the police.* New York: Academic Press.

Blumstein, A., Cohen, J., & Nagin, D. (Eds.). (1978). *Deterrence and incapacitation: Estimating the effects of criminal sanctions on crime rates.* Washington, DC: National Academy of Sciences.

Bograd, M. (1988). Feminist perspectives on wife abuse: An introduction. In K. Yllo & M. Bograd (Eds.), *Feminist perspectives on wife abuse*. Newbury Park, CA: Sage.

Bowker, L. H. (1982). Police services to battered women. *Criminal Justice and Behavior, 9*(4), 476-494.

Boyer, P. (1978). *Urban masses and moral order in America, 1820-1920*. Cambridge, MA: Harvard University Press.

Boyle, C. (1980, Spring). Violence against wives—the criminal law in retreat? *Northern Ireland Quarterly, 31*, 565-586.

Breedlove, R. et al. (1988). Domestic violence and the police: Kansas City. In *The law enforcement response to family violence* (Manual). New York: Victim Services Agency.

Breedlove, R., Sandker, D. M., Kennish, J. W., & Sawtell, R. K. (1977). Domestic violence and the police: Kansas City. In M. Wilt & J. Bannon (Eds.), *Domestic violence and the police: Studies in Detroit and Kansas City*. Washington, DC: The Police Foundation.

Brown, S. (1984). Police responses to wife beating: Neglect of a crime of violence. *Journal of Criminal Justice, 12*, 277-288.

Buchanan, D., & Perry, P. (1985). Attitudes of police recruits towards domestic disturbances: An evaluation of family crisis intervention training. *Journal of Criminal Justice, 13*, 561-572.

Burris, C. A., & Jaffe, P. (1983). Wife abuse as a crime: The impact of police laying charges. *Canadian Journal of Criminology, 25*, 309-318.

Buzawa, E. (1978). *Traditional responses to domestic disturbances*. Paper presented at Michigan Sociological Association, Detroit.

Buzawa, E. (1979). Legislative responses to the problem of domestic violence in Michigan. *Wayne Law Review,25*(3), 859-881.

Buzawa, E. (1981, June). The role of race in predicting patrol officer job satisfaction. *Journal of Criminal Justice, 9*, 63-77.

Buzawa, E. (1982). Police officer response to domestic violence legislation in Michigan. *Journal of Police Science and Administration, 10*(4), 415-424.

Buzawa, E. (1988). Explaining variations in police response to domestic violence: A case study in Detroit and New England. In G. Hotaling, D. Kinkelhor, J. T. Kirkpatrick, & M. A. Straus, *Coping with family violence: Research and policy perspectives.*. Newbury Park, CA: Sage.

Buzawa, E., & Buzawa, C. (1985). Legislative trends in the criminal justice response to domestic violence. In A. Lincoln & M. Straus (Eds.), *Crime and the family*. New York: Charles C Thomas.

Buzawa, E., & Buzawa, C. (Eds.). (1990). *Domestic violence: The criminal justice response*. Westport, CT: Greenwood Press.

Cannavale, F. (1976). *Witness cooperation*. Lexington, MA: Lexington Books.

Cannavale, F., & Falcon, W. (1986). *Improving witness cooperation*. Washington, DC: U.S. Government Printing Office.

Carmody, D. C., & Williams, K. R. (1987). Wife assault and perceptions of sanctions. *Violence and Victims, 2*(1): 25-39.

Coates, C. J., & Leong, D. J. (1980). *Conflict and communication for women and men in battering relationships*. Denver Anti-Crime Council. Washington, DC: U.S. Department of Justice, LEAA.

Cole, G. (1984). The decision to prosecute. In George Cole (Ed.), *Criminal justice: Law and politics* (5th ed.). Monterey, CA: Brooks/ Cole.

Davis, P. (1983). Restoring the semblance of order: Police strategies in the domestic disturbance. *Symbolic Interaction, 6*(2), 261-278.

Deschner, J. (1984). *The hitting habit: Anger control for battering couples*. New York: Free Press.

Dobash, R. E., & Dobash, R. (1979). *Violence against wives: A case against the patriarchy*. New York: Free Press.

Dolon, R., Hendricks, J., & Meagher, M. S. (1986). Police practices and attitudes toward domestic violence. *Journal of Police Science and Administration, 14*(3), 187-192.

Dutton, D. (1988). *The domestic assault of women: Psychological and criminal justice perspectives.* Boston: Allyn & Bacon.

Dutton, D. (1987). *The prediction of recidivism in a population of wife assaulters.* Paper presented at the Third International Family Violence Conference, Durham, NH.

Dutton, D. (1986). Wife assaulters' explanations for assault: The neutralization of self-punishment. *Canadian Journal of Behavioral Science, 18*(4), 381-390.

Dutton, D., Hart, D. S., Kennedy, L., & Williams, K. (1990). Arrest and the reduction of repeat wife assault. In E. Buzawa & C. Buzawa (Eds.), *Domestic violence: The criminal justice response.* Westwood, CT: Auburn House.

Dutton, D., & Strachan, C. (1987). *The prediction of recidivism in a population of wife assaulters.* Paper presented at the Third National Conference for Family Violence Researchers, Durham, NH.

Elliott, D. S. (1989). Criminal justice procedures in family violence crimes. In L. Ohlin & M. Tonry (Eds.), *Crime and justice: A review of research* (pp. 427-480). London: University of Chicago Press.

Ellis, J. W. (1984). Prosecutorial discretion to charge in cases of spousal assault: A dialogue. *Journal of Criminal Law and Criminology, 75* (Spring), 56-102.

Eppler, A. (1986). Battered women and the equal protection clause: Will the constitution help them when the police won't? *The Yale Law Journal, 95*, 788-809.

Epstein, S. (1987). The problem of dual arrest in family violence cases. In *The law enforcement response to family violence* (Manual). New York: Victim Services Agency.

Farrington, K. M. (1980). Stress and family violence. In M. A. Straus & G. T. Hotaling (Eds.), *Social causes of husband wife violence* (pp. 94-114). Minneapolis: University of Minnesota Press.

Faulk, R. (1977). Men who assault their wives. In M. Roy (Ed.), *Battered women: A psychosociological study of domestic violence.* New York: Van Nostrand.

Feld, L. S., & Straus, M. (1989). Escalation and desistance of wife assault in marriage. *Criminology, 27*(1), 141-161.

Ferraro, K. (1989a). The legal response to women battering in the United States. In J. Hamner, J. Radford, & E. Stanko (Eds.), *Women, policing, and male violence* (pp. 155-184). London: Routledge & Keegan Paul.

Ferraro, K. (1989b). Policing women battering. *Social Problems, 36*(1), 61-74.

Field, M., & Field, H. (1973). Marital violence and the criminal process: Neither justice nor peace. *Social Service Review, 47*(2), 221-240.

Finesmith, B. K. (1983, Winter). Police response to battered women: A critique and proposals for reform. *Seton Hall Law Review*, pp. 74-109.

Finn, P. (1989). Statutory authority in the use and enforcement of civil protection orders against domestic abuse. *Family Law Quarterly, 24*(1), 43-73.

Ford, D. A. (1990). The preventative impacts of policies for prosecuting wife batterers. In E. Buzawa & C. Buzawa (Eds.), *Domestic violence: The criminal justice response.* Westwood, CT: Auburn House.

Ford, D. A. (1983). Wife battery and criminal justice: A study of victim decision-making. *Family Relations, 32*, 463-475.

Ford, D. A. (1984, August). *Prosecution as a victim power resource for managing conjugal violence.* Version of the paper presented at the annual meeting of the Society for the Study of Social Problems, San Antonio, TX.

Ford, D. A. (1987, July). *The impact of police officers' attitudes toward victims on the disinclination to arrest wife batterers.* Paper presented at the Third International Conference for Family Violence Researchers, Durham, NH.

Ford, D. A. (1988, November). *Preventing wife battery through criminal justice*. Paper presented at the annual meeting of the American Society of Criminology, Chicago, IL.

Ford, D. A., & Burke, M. J. (1987, July). *Victim initiated criminal complaints for wife battery: An assessment of motives*. Paper presented at the Third National Conference for Family Violence Researchers, Durham, NH.

Freeman, M. (1980). Violence against women: Does the legal system provide solutions or itself constitute the problem? *British Journal of Law and Society, 7 (Winter)*, 216-241.

Garner, J. (1990). Alternative police responses to spouse assault: The design of seven field experiments. In E. Buzawa & C. Buzawa (Eds.), *Domestic violence: The criminal justice response*. Westwood, CT: Auburn House.

Garner, J., & Clemmer, E. (1986). Danger to police in domestic disturbances: A new look. In *National Institute of Justice: Research in Brief*. Washington, DC: U.S. Department of Jutsice.

Garner, J., & Visher, C. (1988), September/October). *Policy experiments come of age* (NIJ Rep. No. 211). Washington DC: U.S. Department of Justice.

Gelles, R. J. (1972). *The violent home: A study of physical aggression between husbands and wives*. Beverly Hills, CA: Sage.

Gelles, R., & Straus, M. (1988). *Intimate violence*. New York: Simon & Schuster.

Gelles, R., & Straus, M. A., (1985). Violence in the American family. In A. J. Lincoln & M. A. Straus (Eds.), *Crime in the family* (pp. 88-110). Springfield, IL: Charles C Thomas.

Gibbs, J. (1985). Detterence theory and research. *Nebraska Symposium on Motivation, 33*, 87-130.

Golden, J. F. (1987). Mutual orders of protection in New York state family offense proceedings: A denial of 'liberty' without due process of law. *Columbia Human Rights Law Review, 18*(2), 309-331.

Gondolf, E. W. (1984). *Men who batter: An integrated approach stopping wife abuse*. Homes Beach, FL: Learning Publications.

Goolkasian, G. A. (1986). The judicial system and domestic violence: An expanding role. *Response, 9*(4), 2-7.

Gottfredson, M., & Hirschi, T. (1988). Career criminals and selective incapacitation. In J. E. Scott & T. Hirschi (Eds.), *Controversial issues in crime and justice* (pp. 199-210). Newbury Park, CA: Sage.

Graham, R., Dee, L., Rawlings, E., & Rimini, N. (1988). Survivors of terror: Battered women, hostages and the Stockholm Syndrome. In K. Yllo & M. Bograd (Eds.), *Feminist perspectives on wife abuse* (pp. 217-233). Newbury Park, CA: Sage.

Grau, J., Fagan, J., & Wexler, S. (1985). Restraining orders for battered women: Issues of access and efficacy. In C. Schweber & C. Feinman (Eds.), *Criminal justice politics and women: The aftermath of legally mandated change* (pp. 13-28). New York: Hatworth Press.

Green, H. W. (1984). *Turning fear to hope*. Nashville, TN: Thomas Nelson, Inc.

Greenstein, H. (1982). *Role of mediation in domestic violence cases*. American Bar Association Special Committee on Resolution of Minor Disputes.

Gundle, R. (1986). Civil liability for police failure to arrest: Nearing v. Weaver. *Women's Rights Law Reporter, 3&4*.

Halpern, R. (1984). *Battered women's alternatives: The men's program component*. Paper presented to the American Psychological Association, Toronto, Canada.

Hamberger, K. L., & Hastings, J. H. (1986). *Characteristics of male spouse abusers: Is psychopathology part of the picture?* Paper presented at the American Society of Criminology, Atlanta, GA.

Hammond, N. (1977). *Domestic assault: A report on family violence in Michigan*. State of Michigan.

Hanmer, J., Radford, J., & Stanko, E. (1989). Improving policing for women: The way forward. In J. Hanmer, J. Radford, & E. Stanko (Eds.), *Women, policing and male violence: International perspectives* (pp. 185-201). London: Routledge & Keegan & Paul.

Hanmer, J., Radford, J., & Stanko, E. (1989). Policing men's violence: An introduction. In J. Hanmer, J. Radford, & E. Stanko (Eds.), *Women, policing and male violence: International perspectives* (pp. 1-12). London: Routledge & Keegan Paul.

Hanmer, J., Radford, J., & Stanko, E. (Eds.). (1989). *Women, policing and male violence: International perspectives*. London: Routledge, & Keegan Paul.

Harris, R. N. (1973). *The police academy: An inside view*. New York: John Wiley.

Hart, W., Ashcroft, J., Burgess, A., Flanagan, N., Meese, C., Milton, C., Narramores, C., Oretega, R., & Seward, F. (1984). *Attorney General's Task Force on Family Violence*. Washington, DC: U.S. Government Printing Office.

Hartog, H. (1976). The public law of a county court: Judicial government in eighteenth century Massachusetts. *The American Journal of Legal History, 20*, 282-329.

Hatty, S. (1989). Policing male violence in Australia. In J. Hanmer, J. Radford, & E. Stanko (Eds.), *Women, policing and male violence: International perspectives* (pp. 70-89). London: Routledge & Keegan Paul.

Hawkins, R., & Beauvais, C. (1985). *Evaluation of group therapy with abusive men: The police record*. Paper presented at the American Psychological Association, Los Angeles, CA.

Hendricks, J. (1988). *Domestic violence legislation: A national study status of the states*. Paper presented to the Academy of Criminal Justice Sciences, San Francisco, CA.

Holmes, W., & Bibel, D. (1988). *Police response to domestic violence: Final report*. Prepared for U.S. Bureau of Justice Statistics, Washington, DC.

Homant, J. R., & Kennedy, D. B. (1984). Content analysis of statements about policewomen's handling of domestic violence. *American Journal of Police, 3*(2), 265-283.

Homant, J. R., & Kennedy, D. B., (1985). Police perceptions of spouse abuse: A comparison of male and female officers. *Journal of Criminal Justice, 13*(1), 29-47.

Hotaling, & G. T., Straus, M. A., with Lincoln, A. (1989). Intrafamily violence and crime and violence outside the family. In L. Ohlin & M. Tonry (Eds.), *Family violence* (pp. 315-376). Chicago: University of Chicago Press.

Hotaling, G. T., & Sugarman, D. B. (1986). An analysis of risk makers in husband to wife violence: The current state of knowledge. *Violence and Victims, 1*(2), 101-124.

Hotaling, G. T., & Sugarman, D. B. (1990). The primary prevention of wife assault. In R. T. Ammerman & M. Herson (Eds.), *Treatment of family violence: A source book*. New York: John Wiley.

Jacoby, J. (1980). *The American prosecutor: A search for identity*. Lexington, MA: Lexington Books.

Jaffe, P., et al. (1986). The impact of police charges in incidents of wife abuse. *Journal of Family Violence, 1*, 37-49.

Jaffe, P., Wilson, S., & Wolfe, D. (1986). Promoting changes in attitudes and understanding of conflict resolution among child witnesses of family violence. *Canadian Journal of Behavioral Science Review, 18*(4), 356-366.

Jolin, A. (1983). Domestic violence legislation: An impact assessment. *Journal of Police Science and Administration, 11*(4), 451-456.

Kantor, G. K. & Straus, M. (1987). The 'drunken bum' theory of wife beating. *Social Problems, 34*(3), 213-230.

Kemp, C. H., Silverman, F. N., Steele, B. F., Droegenmuller, W., & Silver, H. (1962). The battered child syndrome. *Journal of the American Medical Association, 181*, 17-24.

Koehler, L. K. (1980). *Women of the republic: Intellect and ideology in revolutionary America*. Chapel Hill: University of North Carolina Press.

Labaton, S. (1989, December 29). New tactics in the war on drugs tilt scales of justice off balance. *The New York Times*.

Langan, P., & Innes, C. (1986). *Preventing domestic violence against women*. Bureau of Justice Statistics. Washington, DC: U.S. Department of Justice.

Langley, R., & Levy, R. (1977). *Wife beating: The silent crisis.* New York: Dutton.

Langley, R., & Levy, R. (1978). Wife abuse and the police response. *FBI Law Enforcement Bulletin, 47,* 4-9.

Lawrenz, F., Lembo, R., & Schade, S. (1988). Time series analysis of the effect of a domestic violence directive on the number of arrests per day. *Journal of Criminal Justice, 16,* 493-498.

Lempert, R. (1987, June 21). Spouse abuse: Ann Arbor rushed into arrest ordinance without studying side effects. *Ann Arbor News.*

Lempert, R. (1989). Humility is a virtue: On the publicization of policy relevant research. *Law and Society Review, 23,* 145-161.

Lerman, L. (1981). *Prosecution of spouse abuse innovations in criminal jutsice response.* Washington, DC: Center for Women Policy Studies.

Lerman, L. (1982). Expansion of arrest power: A key to effective intervention. *Vermont Law Review, 7,* 59-70.

Lerman, L. (1984). Mediation of wife abuse cases: The adverse impact of informal dispute resolution of women. *Harvard Women's Law Journal, 7,* 65-67.

Levinson, D. (1989). *Family violence in cross cultural perspective.* Newbury Park, CA: Sage

Liebman, D., & Schwartz, J. (1973). Police programs in domestic crisis intervention: A review. In J. R. Snibbe & H. M. Snibbe (Eds.), *The urban policeman in transition.* Springfield, IL: Charles C Thomas.

Loving. (1980). *Responding to spouse abuse and wife beating: A guide for police.* Washington, DC: Police Executive Research Forum.

Loving, N., & Quirk, M. (1982). Spouse abuse: The need for new law enforcement responses. *FBI Law Enforcement Bulletin, 51*(12), 10-16.

Manning, P. (1977). *Police work: The sociological organization of policing.* Cambridge: MIT Press.

Manning, P. (1978). The police: Mandate, strategies and appearances. In P. Manning & J. Von Mannen (Eds.), *Policing: A view from the street.* Santa Monica, CA: Goodyear Publishing.

Manning, P., & Van Maanen, J. (Eds.). (1978). *Policing: A view from the street.* Santa Monica, CA: Goodyear Publications.

Martin, D. (1976). *Battered wives.* San Francisco, CA: Glide Publications.

Martin, D. (1978). Battered women: Society's problem. In J. R. Chapman & M. Gates (Eds.), *The victimization of women* (pp. 111-141). Beverly Hills, CA: Sage.

Martin, D. (1979). What keeps a woman captive in a violent relationship?: The social context of battering. In D. M. Moore (Ed.), *Battered women* (pp. 33-57). Beverly Hills, CA: Sage.

Martin, D. (1985). Domestic violence: A sociological perspectives. In D. J. Sonkin, D. Martin, & L. E. Walker (Eds.), *Male batterer* (pp. 1-32). New York: Springer.

McLeod, M. (1983). Victim noncooperation in the prosecution of domestic assault. *Criminology, 21*(3), 395-416.

McLeod, M. (1984). Women against men: An examination of domestic violence based on an analysis of official data and national victimization data. *Justice Quarterly, 1*(1), 171-192.

NADA (1980). *Prosecutor's responsibility in spouse abuse cases.* National District Attorneys Association. National Criminal Justice Reference Service.

National Clearinghouse on Domestic Violence (1980). *Battered women: A national concern.* Rockville, MD: Author.

Ohlin, L., & Tonry, M. (1989). *Family violence. Crime and justice: A review of research (Vol. 11).* Chicago: University of Chicago Press.

Oppenlander, N. (1982). Coping or copping out: Police service delivery in domestic disputes. *Criminology, 20*(3), 449-465.

Pagelow, D. M. (1984). *Family violence.* New York: Praeger.

Pahl, J. (1985). *Private violence and public policy: The needs of battered women and the response of the public services.* London: Routledge & Kegan Paul.

Parnas, R. I. (1967). The police response to the domestic disturbance. *Wisconsin Law Review, 2,* 914-60.

Parnas, R. I. (1970). Judicial response to intra-family violence. *Minnesota Law Review, 54,* 585-644.

Parnas, R. I. (1971). Police discretion and diversion of incidents of intra-family violence. *Law & Contemporary Problems, 36.*

Parnas, R. I. (1973). Prosecutorial and judicial handling of family violence. *Criminal Law Bulletin, 9,* 733-769.

Parnas, R. I. (1978). The relevance of criminal law to interspousal violence. In J. Eekelaar & K. Katz (Eds.), *Family Violence, 188,* 190-91.

Pasternoster, R. (1987). The deterrent effect of the perceived certainty and severity of punishment: A review of the evidence and issues. *Justice Quarterly, 4,* 173-217.

Pastoor, M. K. (1984). Police training and the effectiveness of Minnesota 'Domestic Abuse' laws. *Law and Inequality, 2,* 557-607.

Pepinsky, H. E. (1976). Police patrolman's offense-reporting behavior. *Journal of Research in Crime and Delinquency, 13*(1), 33-47.

Pierce, G. (in press). Toward a surveillance system for assaultive injuries. In E. Buzawa & C. Buzawa (Eds.), *Domestic violence: The criminal justice response.* Westwood, CT: Auburn House.

Pierce, G. L. (1984, July). *The police and domestic violence: The need to coordinate community resources.* Paper presented to the Governor's Anti-Crime Council, Boston, MA.

Pierce, G., & Deutsch, S. (1990). Do police actions and responses to domestic violence calls make a difference? A quasi experimental analysis. *Journal of Quantitative Criminology.*

Pierce, G., Spaar, S., & Briggs, B. (1988, November). Character of calls for police work. *NIJ Report.*

Pirog-Good, M. A., & Stets, J. (1986). Program for abusers: Who drops out and what can be done. *Response, 9*(2), 17-19.

Pirro, J. (1982). Domestic violence: The criminal court response. *New York State Bar Journal, 54,*(6), pp. 352-357.

Pleck, E. (1979). Wife beating in nineteenth century America. *Victimology, 4*(1), 60-74.

Pleck, E. (1989). Criminal approaches to family violence 1640-1980. In L. Ohlin & M. Tonry, (Eds.), *Crime and justice: A review of research, Vol. 11* (pp. 19-58.) Chicago: University of Chicago Press.

President's Commission on Law Enforcement and the Administration of Justice. (1967). *Task force report: The police.* Washington, DC: U.S. Government Printing Office.

Punch, M. (1985). *Conduct unbecoming.* London: MacMillan.

Quarm, D., & Schwartz, M. (1983). Legal reform and the criminal court: The case of domestic violence. *Northern Kentucky Law Review, 10,* 199-225.

Quinn, D. (1985). Ex parte protection orders: Is due process locked out? *Temple Law Quarterly, 58,* 843-872.

Radford, J. (1989). Women and policing: Contradictions old and new. In J. Hanmer, J. Radford, & B. Stanko (Eds.), *Women, policing and male violence* (pp. 13-45). London: Routledge & Keegan Paul.

Ray, L. (1982). Domestic violence mediation demands careful screening. In *Alternative means of family dispute resolution* (pp. 417-427). Washington, DC:NP

Reed, D., Fischer, S., Kantootr, G., & Karales, K. (1983). *All they can do . . . Police response to battered women's complaints.* Chicago: Chicago Law Enforcement Study Group.

Reis, A. J. (1971). *The police and the public.* New Haven, CT: Yale University Press.

Rothman, D. J. (1980). *Conscience and convenience: The asylum and its alternatives in progressive America.* Boston, MA: Little, Brown.

Roy, M. (Ed.). (1977). *Battered women: A psychosociological study of domestic violence*. New York: Van Nostrand Reinhold.

Saunders, D. G., & Size, P. B. (1986). Attitudes about woman abuse among police officers, victims and victim advocates. *Journal of Interpersonal Violence, 1*, 24-42.

Schechter, S. (1982). *Women and male violence: The visions and struggle of the battered women's movement*. Boston, MA: South End Press.

Schmidt, J., & Steury, E. H. (1989). Prosecutorial discretion in filing charges in domestic violence cases. *Criminology, 27*(3), 487-510.

Sherman, L. W., & Berk, R. A. (1984). The specific deterrent effects of arrest for domestic assault. *American Sociological Review, 49*, 261-272.

Sherman, L. W., & Cohn, E. G. (1989). The impact of research on legal policy: The Minneapolis Domestic Violence Experiment. *Law and Society Review, 23*(1), 117-144.

Skolnick, J. H. (1975). *Justice without trial*. New York: John Wiley.

Skogan, W. (1981). *Issues in the measurement of victimization*. Washington, DC: U.S. Government Printing Office.

Smith, B. E. (1979). *The prosecutor's witness: An urban suburban comparison*. Unpublished dissertation.

Smith, B. E. (1983). *Non-stranger violence. The criminal court's response*. Washington, DC: U.S. Department of Justice, N.I.J.

Snell, J. E., et al. (1964). The wife beater's wife: A study of family interaction. *Archives of General Psychiatry 11*, 107-113.

Sonkin, D., Martin, D., & Walker, L. E. (1985). *Group treatment for men who batter women*. New York: Singer Press.

Stallone, D. R. (1984). Decriminalization of violence in the home: Mediation in wife battering cases. *Law and Inequality, 2*, 493-505.

Stanko, E. A. (1982). Would you believe this woman? In N. H. Rafter & E. A. Stanko (Eds.), *Judge, lawyer, victim, thief: Women, gender roles and criminal justice*. Boston, MA: Northeastern University Press.

Stanko, E. A. (1989). Missing the mark? Police battering. In J. Hanmer, J. Radford & B. Stanko (Eds.), *Women, policing and male violence* (pp. 46-49). London: Routledge& Keegan Paul.

Star, B. (1982). *Helping the abuser—Intervening effectively in family violence*. Family Service Association of America. New York: National Institute of Justice/National Criminal Justice Reference Service Microfiche Program.

Steinmetz, S. K. (1977). Wifebeating, husbandbeating: A comparison of the use of physical violence between spouses to resolve marital rights. In M. Roy (Ed.), *Battered women: A psychosociological study of domestic violence*. New York: Van Nostrand Reinhold.

Steinmetz, S. K. (1980). Violence prone families. *Annals of the New York Academy of Sciences, 347*, 351-265.

Straus, M. A. (1977-1978). Wife beating: How common and why? *Victimology: An International Journal, 2*(3-4), 443-458.

Straus, M. A. (1980). Wife beating: How common and why. In M. A. Straus & G. T. Hotaling (Eds.), *Social causes of husband wife violence*. Minneapolis: University of Minneapolis Press.

Straus, M. A. (1986a). Medical care costs of intrafamily assault and homicide. *Bulletin of the New York Academy of Medicine, 6*(5), 556-561.

Straus, M. A. (1986b). Domestic violence and homicide antecedents. *Bulletin of New York Academy of Medicine, 62*(5), 446-465.

Straus, M. A., Gelles, R. J., & Steinmetz, S. K. (1980). *Behind closed door: Violence in the American family*. Garden City, NY: Anchor Books.

Straus, M., & Gelles, R. (1986). Social change and change in family violence from 1971 to 1985 as revealed by two national surveys. *Journal of Marriage and the Family, 48*, 465-479.

Straus, M. A., & Hotaling, G. T. (Eds.). (1980). *Social causes of husband wife violence.* Minneapolis: University of Minneapolis Press.

Sugarman, P. B., & Hotaling, G. T. (1989). Violent men in intimate relationships: An analysis of risk markers. *Journal of Applied Social Psychology, 19*(12), 1034-1048.

U.S. Attorney General's Task Force on Family Violence. (1984). *Final Report.* Washington, DC: U.S. Attorney General.

U.S. Commission of Civil Rights. (1978). *Battered women: Issues of public policy.* Washington, DC: U.S. Government Printing Office.

U.S. Commission on Civil Rights. (1982). *Under the rule of thumb: Battered women and the administration of justice.* Washington, DC: National Institute of Justice.

Van Maanen, J. (1973). Observations on the making of policemen. *Human Organization, 32*(4), 407-17.

Van Maanen, J. (1974). Working the street: A developmental view of police behavior. In H. Jacob (Ed.), *The potential for reform of criminal justice* (pp. 83-130). Beverly Hills, CA: Sage.

Van Maanen, J. (1975). Police socialization: A longitudinal examination of job attitudes in an urban police department. *Administrative Science Quarterly, 20,* 207-228.

Van Maanen, J. (1978). Observations on the making of policemen. In P. Manning and J. Van Maanen (Eds.), *Policing: A view from the street.* Santa Monica, CA: Goodyear Publishing.

Vera Institute of Justice (1977). *Felony arrests: Their prosecution and disposition in New York City's courts.* New York: Vera Institute of Justice.

Victim Services Agency. (1988). *The law enforcement response to family violence: A state by state guide to family violence legislation.* New York: Victim Services Agency.

Von Hirsch, A. (1985). *Past or future crimes: Deservedness and dangerousness in the sentencing of criminals.* New Brunswick, NJ: Rutgers University Press.

Waaland, P., & Keeley, S. (1985). Police decision making in wife abuse: The impact of legal and extralegal factors. *Law and Human Behavior, 9*(4), 355-366.

Waits, K. (1985). The criminal justice system's response to battering: Understanding the problem, forging the solutions. *Washington Law Review, 60, 267-329.*

Walker, L. (1979). *Battered women.* New York: Harper & Row.

Westley, W. (1970). *Violence and the police: A sociological study of law, custom and morality.* Cambridge: MIT Press.

Williams, K. (1976). The effects of victim characteristics on violent crimes. In W. F. McDonald (Ed.), *Criminal justice and the victim* (pp. 177-213). Beverly Hills, CA: Sage.

Williams, K. (1978). *The role of the victim in the prosecution of violent crime.* Washington, DC: Institute for Law and Social Research.

Williams, K. R., & Hawkins, R. (1989). The meaning of arrest for wife assault. *Criminology, 27*(1), 163-181.

Wilt, M., & Bannon, J. (1977). *Domestic violence and the police: Studies in Detroit and Kansas City.* Washington, D.C.: The Police Foundation.

Wolfgang, M. (1958). *Patterns of criminal homicide.* Philadelphia: University of Pennsylvania Press.

Worden, R. E., & Pollitz, A. A. (1984). Police arrests in domestic disturbances: A further look. *Law and Society Review, 18,* 105-119.

Yllo, K. (1988). Political and methodological debates in wife abuse research. In K. Yllo & M. Bograd (Eds.), *Feminist perspectives on wife abuse* (pp. 28-50). Newbury Park, CA: Sage.

Zoomer, O. J. (1989). Policing women beating in the Netherlands. In J. Hanmer, J. Radford, & B. Stanko (Eds.), *Women, policing and male violence* (pp. 125-154). London: Routledge & Keegan Paul.

Index

About the Authors

Eve Buzawa received her BA in sociology from the University of Rochester and her MA and Ph.D. from Michigan State University in criminal justice. She is currently an Associate Professor in the Department of Criminal Justice at the University of Lowell, Lowell, Massachusetts. In the area of domestic violence, she has worked at developing and assisting in the administration of domestic violence treatment programs as well as police department policies and training programs in a variety of jurisdictions. She has conducted research and written in this area for several years.

Carl Buzawa received his BA from the University of Rochester in history and political science, his MA from the University of Michigan in political science, and his JD from Harvard Law School. He has been in full-time law practice since 1976 and has taught various law classes on a part-time basis. He has co-authored several articles and chapters in books on the topic of domestic violence.